THE CURIOU

"The brilliant and entertainin
a clear and enjoyable text that .... *.... .... thought*
about the world and our place in it."

LORD REES
Astronomer Royal, President of the Royal Society 2005–2010

"Too often science and faith are pitted against each other. This book breaks down that split in a creative and engaging way. It shows the scope of science in our lives and how the study of science and the study of God feed and magnify each other. Human beings have always been hungry for understanding and meaning, and this book beautifully shows how this has worked out from the earliest time. It is a book that leaves me in awe at the 'art' of science: for the way it unveils the magnificence of God our Creator, who stretches out the canvas."

MOST REVEREND JUSTIN WELBY
Archbishop of Canterbury

"Whether you are at school, retired, or anywhere in between, you cannot help but enjoy The Curious Science Quest books. They ask the 'big questions' about science and meaning, and contain tons of fascinating information, all put into a clear historical context and vividly presented through a clever combination of words and pictures.

Hosted by a tortoise and a cat, you will travel through time. You will laugh, be stimulated, and be enchanted by the wonderful illustrations. The books are a delight in every way."

DR ALLAN CHAPMAN
Historian of astronomy and medicine at the University of Oxford

"A witty and accessible treasure trove of scientific discoveries that goes to the heart of our human quest to understand who we are. This book doesn't dumb down or gloss over imponderables but will leave you marvelling at the science and asking for more."

PROFESSOR REBECCA FITZGERALD
Director of Medical Studies, University of Cambridge
Lister Prize Fellowship (2008), NHS Innovation (2011), NIHR
Research Professorship (2013)

"Has the bug bitten you? Are you curious? Curious to know how the universe evolved from the Big Bang? How matter arranges itself into objects ranging from atomic nuclei to human beings, planets,and stars? Are you curious to know why all these things are the way they are?

Science is good for the 'how' questions but does not necessarily have the answers on the 'why' questions. Can science and religion talk to each other? Enjoy this series and learn more about science and the enriching dialogue between science and faith."

PROFESSOR ROLF HEUER
Director General of CERN from 2009 to 2015
President of the German Physical Society and President of the
SESAME Council

"Here is a wonderful and wittily written introduction to science as the art of asking open questions and not jumping to conclusions. It's also an amusing excursion through evolution and anthropology which packs in a lot of learning with the lightest of touches. A much-needed antidote to the bludgeoning crudity of so much writing in both science and religion."

REVEREND DOCTOR MALCOLM GUITE
Poet, singer-songwriter, priest, and academic
Chaplain at Girton College Cambridge

THE CURIOUS SCIENCE QUEST

MODERN FLIGHTS

WHERE NEXT?

JULIA GOLDING

WITH ANDREW BRIGGS AND ROGER WAGNER

ILLUSTRATIONS BRETT HUDSON

LION
CHILDREN'S

Text copyright © 2019 Julia Golding, Andrew Briggs, and Roger Wagner
Illustrations copyright © 2019 Brett Hudson
This edition copyright © 2019 Lion Hudson IP Limited

The right of Julia Golding, Andrew Briggs, and Roger Wagner to be identified
as the authors and of Brett Hudson to be identified as the illustrator of this
work has been asserted by them in accordance with the Copyright, Designs
and Patents Act 1988.

All rights reserved. No part of this publication may be reproduced or
transmitted in any form or by any means, electronic or mechanical, including
photocopy, recording, or any information storage and retrieval system, without
permission in writing from the publisher.

Published by
Lion Hudson Limited
Wilkinson House, Jordan Hill Business Park, Banbury Road,
Oxford OX2 8DR, England
www.lionhudson.com

ISBN 978 0 7459 7755 3
e-ISBN 978 07459 7802 4

First edition 2019

Acknowledgments
This publication was made possible through the support of a grant from
Templeton Religion Trust. The opinions expressed in this publication are those
of the authors and do not necessarily reflect the views of Templeton Religion
Trust.

A catalogue record for this book is available from the British Library

Printed and bound in the UK, May 2019, LH26

CONTENTS

INTRODUCTION

Life is full of big questions; what we might call *ultimate* questions. In the first five parts of *The Curious Science Quest* our intrepid time travellers, Harriet and Milton, explored some of the most important mysteries:

- When did humans start to ask questions?
- Who were the first scientists?
- What is our place in the solar system?
- What are the laws of the universe?
- Where did we come from?

STOP BUGGING ME!

They have met many curious people, starting with cave painters and then heading to the first scientists in Ancient Greece. From there they travelled on to visit Islamic scholars and medieval monks, then narrowly avoided the Black Death that temporarily put science on pause. They journeyed on to the sixteenth century to see Copernicus, the first thinker in modern times to suggest the earth went around the sun. Next stop was in the seventeenth century to meet the stargazers Kepler and Galileo.

Have you been keeping up?

Things were only just getting going for science at this point because then they hopped over to London to visit the Royal Society men Boyle, Hooke, and Newton. After another plague and the Great Fire, they ended up at the end of the eighteenth century in the observatory of William and Caroline Herschel, a brother-and-sister team of astronomers. They declared that the scientific revolution was well and truly underway.

Their last stop was with the inquisitive people of the nineteenth century, where they headed out on Victorian voyages of discovery – on the beach, down a coal mine, on a steam train, and even in a sewer!

We left them standing outside the laboratory of one of the founders of the atomic age. But watch out: things are about to go radioactive!

Our Time Travelling Guides

Meet our guides to the ultimate questions.

Harriet is a tortoise. She was collected by Charles Darwin on his famous voyage on the *Beagle* (1831–36), which was when he explored the world and saw many things that led him to the Theory of Evolution. Harriet was brought back in his suitcase to England to be the family pet. As a tortoise she can live for a very long time and is well over a hundred.

Harriet

Milton is a cat. He belongs to the famous twentieth-century physicist, Erwin Schrödinger, and inspired some of his owner's best ideas. Milton is not very good at making up his mind.

Milton

Curious Quest

Having noticed some curious words over the entrance to a famous laboratory in Cambridge University, Harriet and Milton decided to go on a quest to find out the answers to as many ultimate questions as they can. In fact, they agreed to travel in time to see some of the most important events in the history of science.

*The works of the Lord are great,
sought out of all them that have pleasure therein*

In this series, you are invited to go with them. But look out for the Curiosity Bug hidden in some intriguing places. See how many of these you can count. Answer on page 127.

Harriet and Milton are now on the final part of their quest to ask, "Where is science leading us in the future?" That might be the most curious question of all!

The Curiosity Bug

Atomic Heroes and Radioactivity

The year is 1911. Harriet and Milton, dressed in protective hazmat suits, are peering through the window of the door of Marie Skłowdowska-Curie's laboratory in Paris. Harriet had warned Milton before leaving the time machine that the dangers of radioactivity weren't well understood when it was first discovered. Marie and the other scientists are handling their sample with bare hands, which people now know *never* to do.

Milton raises his paw to knock but Harriet holds him back.

"Wait, Milton. Before we go in to the danger zone to meet one of my heroes, I think we need to get up to speed with the story of atomic science – that's the study of the smallest things."

Milton wants to get on with the adventure. There are interesting noises and smells coming from inside the laboratory. "Really, Harriet? I've travelled from Ancient Greece to Paris in 1911, visiting nearly all the most famous scientists on the way: what else do I need to know?" He is scratching at the door and mewing like he does when he wants his bowl of cat food. If Harriet doesn't hurry with her story, someone will hear and let them in before they're ready to understand what is going on inside.

"We mustn't get ahead of ourselves…"

"I thought that was what we were always doing in the time machine!"

She laughs. "True – you have a point. But there's so much to tell in the modern story of science because it rapidly gets more complicated and specialized." Thinking quickly, Harriet realizes how to attract Milton's attention. "In the case of atomic science, though, it starts with plum pudding."

Milton stops scratching. "Oh! This sounds very hopeful." He sits down expectantly, his mouth watering.

"Here: have a look at this."

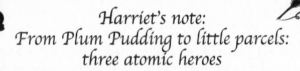

Harriet's note:
From Plum Pudding to little parcels: three atomic heroes

During the nineteenth century, chemists worked on building the periodic table – their way of organizing all the known elements into similar groups.

Elements are substances that cannot be broken down into simpler forms by chemical means, e.g. hydrogen, oxygen, gold.

Chemists have been filling in the gaps ever since. The element with the atomic number 1 (hydrogen) goes at the top of the chart, with 118 (Oganesson – an element only made in the laboratory, not found in nature) at the bottom, a bit like organizing the kitchen cupboard so you know where to put your hand on something!

The problem was that the chemists didn't know what an atom was made of! They needed the help of three atomic age heroes.

The first of our atomic men, J. J. Thomson (1856–1940), a Cambridge scientist, came along to help with his Plum Pudding model. While experimenting with a piece of laboratory equipment called a cathode ray tube, he detected little corpuscles, or particles, which he called "electrons", in the atoms. He realized that atoms themselves were made up of other even smaller things. He imagined atoms were a mixture of spread-out positive charge and particles of negative charge evenly distributed among the positive charge like dried fruit in a pudding.

It was a useful if not accurate picture because it led his student Ernest Rutherford (1873–1937), a New Zealander, to continue experimenting. The second of our atomic scientists noticed two kinds of rays that he could not identify coming from an element called uranium. He gave them the names alpha and beta (A and B in the Greek alphabet). He devised a clever idea to test what was going on inside the atom: he bombarded a sheet of gold foil with the alpha rays.

He was amazed by what he discovered, calling it the most incredible event of his life. He saw that while the alpha ray usually passed through the foil, sometimes it bounced back. This led him to conclude that the Plum Pudding Model could not be true, and that an atom had a really dense nucleus surrounded by a lot of space. Some of his rays were hitting the nucleus and bouncing back, while most travelled through. He'd already earned a Nobel Prize in 1908 for other work, but after this discovery he was known as the founder of nuclear physics.

Enter hero number three, a Danish scientist called Niels Bohr (1885–1962). This atomic hero came up with three very helpful conclusions from his detective work:

1. A better model than plum pudding is the solar system with the nucleus at the centre like the sun, with orbiting electrons.

2. The electrons can only be in certain orbits around the nucleus.

3. Electrons can change orbits by taking in or giving off radiation in fixed amounts called quanta, an idea that helped to establish the field of quantum physics. (You can think of it a little like a spaceship giving a burst of the engine to move it into a higher or lower orbit.) [1]

---

1 Quantum means "little parcel" in Latin and was first used by another great scientist, Max Planck, in 1900. We'll find out more about this in chapter 2.

The most curious thing about this is that everything we see and touch is made up of atoms that are mostly empty space!

"That's very curious," says Milton. "You know my master, Schrödinger, works on atoms?" Harriet nods. Milton has the good fortune to belong to one of the twentieth century's cleverest men. "Well, what I've always wondered when I've heard him talking is this: if most of an atom is empty, why does anything appear solid?" He raps on the wooden door to prove his point.

"That is an excellent question, Milton," agrees Harriet. "The answer is that the pictures we are talking about – plum puddings and solar systems – can mislead us to taking them too literally. Natural laws seem to act differently at the quantum, or very smallest, level, so it is easy for us to go wrong."

"So the space isn't really empty?" Milton wrinkles his whiskers in thought.

"Only when we are imagining an atom as if it's unmoving, like a diagram of the solar system; but electrons in an atom dance around the nucleus all the time super-fast. Another image that might help is to picture an atom like a swarm of bees. The bees, or electrons, are moving around so fast that the swarm makes a shape that is the sum total of all the little insects."

"I wouldn't touch a swarm…"

"I should hope not!"

"But what makes an atom solid, then?"

"Our bee-like electrons are full of energy. When we touch them they push back, making what we touch feel 'solid'. Again this is a picture, but it's not a bad one to describe how the forces inside an atom work."

"I think I'd better look into this some more," says Milton. "It's fascinating stuff."

"You are turning into a real scientific explorer, Milton." Harriet is so proud of him. "I have to admit I've told you all I know. When we get back to quantum physics later on our quest, maybe you can tell me what you found out?"

Milton puffs out his chest, pleased with the responsibility. "I will!"

Never trust an atom – they make up everything!

The door opens and a lady in a long dress looks down at them.

"I was right: I thought I heard knocking. Who are you two?"

Fortunately, the time travellers are hidden by their hazmat suits. They both stand on their back legs to look as human as possible.

"Visitors," says Harriet.

"Very small ones," adds Milton. He tucks his tail out of sight. "On a school trip."

"We've heard exciting things about your work so we've come to see what you are doing," continues Harriet.

Marie Skłodowska-Curie opens the door wider. "Then you'd better come in, children. Why are you dressed like that?"

"Um…" says Harriet.

"It's the fashion where we come from," replies Milton quickly.

"How odd." The scientist guides them into her workroom. "But let me show you what we're doing. Today we are extracting radioactive uranium from pitchblende. That's the black material on the workbench. Miners digging up uranium in places like Cornwall in England sometimes find seams of it underground and send it to me as they know I find it very useful. It is full of fascinating elements."

"What does radioactive mean, madame?" asks Milton. He doesn't fancy getting too close to the pitchblende.

"Please, call me Marie." She picks up the rock, quite unafraid to handle it. "Radioactivity is a new idea – I'm not surprised you don't know. The first hint we got about radioactivity was when a talented German scientist, Wilhelm Röntgen, discovered X-rays by mistake. He was doing another experiment and saw that some photographic paper across the laboratory had changed colour."

"That must've seemed odd," says Harriet.

"Indeed," agrees Marie. "Another scientist might've ignored it, or put it down to accident, but Röntgen decided to ask more questions. He realized the new rays coming from his experiment could pass through things without being reflected or bent and had reached the paper. He began to test out his idea and even took an image of his wife's hand with the new rays. You can see the bones and her wedding ring, but no skin or flesh."

"Ooh, spooky!" says Milton.

Marie smiles. "Not so much spooky as spectacular! That led us to realize that these new X-rays would be very useful for doctors. You can see inside the body."

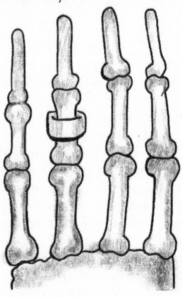

"What happened next?" asks Harriet.

"The story then comes here to Paris. Henri Becquerel was studying the light, or fluorescence, that comes off uranium. He realized that it was different from X-rays. My husband, Pierre, and I became fascinated by this and carried on working on the mystery. Pierre died in an accident a few years ago and I've had to carry on my research without him since then. I was the one who coined the term 'radioactive' to describe what is happening to the uranium. It seems to be catching on in scientific circles."

"So what is happening to the uranium?" asks Milton.

"Ah, that's the most curious thing." Marie shows them her samples set out on the laboratory desk. "It's like the dreams of the alchemists so many centuries ago. They wanted to change one element into another in their search for gold. Here we have uranium, which is slowly losing particles and turning into lead. We didn't know this was possible until now and it is changing how we thinking about elements."

"How exciting!" exclaims Milton.

"I've also discovered two other new elements – thorium and polonium. That last one I named after the country where I was born, Poland," she adds proudly.

"And she goes on to be the first woman to get a Nobel Prize, and the first person to be awarded two Nobel Prizes, for her scientific work," Harriet whispers to Milton.

Fortunately, Marie doesn't hear the whispers. "I think radioactive substances will prove very useful to doctors as they can cross physical barriers. Perhaps they will even help cure cancer…?"

Looking around her workplace, Milton is worried that Marie isn't taking enough care of herself. "Might they not also be very dangerous?"

Harriet steps on his tail. "You mustn't interfere with the timeline!" she hisses. "Even when we want to."

"I suppose they might," says Marie. "We'll need to test this in the laboratory." The scientist looks at her watch. "I'm afraid I'll have to cut this short. I have to get back to my children for dinner time."

"Thank you for your time. It was a pleasure meeting you," says Harriet.

The time travellers hurry back into the time machine.

"Marie might be the first working-mother scientist," says Harriet with a sigh as they watch her leave the laboratory for the day.

"She is a very impressive lady," agrees Milton.

"Her daughter, Irène, follows her into science and you are right about the health hazards. Tragically both Marie and Irène die young of blood cancer brought on by the unsafe working conditions. The dangers of handling radioactive materials were not understood until much later."

"I suppose a good lesson to learn is to always obey safety instructions in the school laboratory," muses Milton.

"That's right. Things that look harmless can turn out to be deadly."

Milton tries to lift the mood as the machine whirrs into life. "I've heard that lots of natural objects are radioactive."

"Oh yes – like what?" Harriet isn't really paying attention.

"Bananas."

That stops her in her tracks. "Bananas?"

"It's true. That's because they have a special form of the element potassium in them – and that's a little radioactive."

"I didn't know that," admits Harriet. "Are they safe?" She's quite fond of the fruit.

"Guess how many you would have to eat to get a fatal dose of radioactive poisoning?" asks Milton as Harriet sets the next coordinates for the time machine. "I've looked it up."

Harriet thinks about it a little more. Animals have been eating bananas for millions of years and she's never heard of any deaths. "Thousands?"

"No, ten million – in one go." Milton grins.

"I think my tummy would explode first if I tried that!" says Harriet.

"Exactly. So it is safe to go on eating bananas. It is not possible to eat enough to do any harm from radiation."

"Now we've settled the slippery question of radioactive bananas, are you ready for the next stage in the atomic age?" asks Harriet.

"Yes!" Milton rummages in the food cupboard for a banana for Harriet and a sardine for himself. All this talk of them has made him hungry. It would be a good idea to have a snack to carry them over until dinner time.

"It involves a very big question to do with right and wrong," she adds.

Milton emerges triumphant from the cupboard, waving a banana. He feels fairly confident his experience on the Curiosity Quest has prepared him for everything. "OK, let's go. I'm ready for anything."

Atomic bombs and the Manhattan Project

The time machine lands in July 1945 in New Mexico, USA. Milton begins to take off his hazmat suit because it looks very hot outside. The sun beats down on the desert and a heat haze shimmers on the horizon.

"Leave the suit on," cautions Harriet.

They exit the machine and find themselves among a group of observers watching the desert.

"What's going on?" whispers Milton. What could they all be doing looking so expectantly into the distance? "Camel racing?"

"We're in America, Milton! No camel racing. We're here for the first ever test of a nuclear weapon."

Milton is getting fidgety. He doesn't mind laboratories but military experiments sound a different thing altogether. "Harriet, I thought this was the Curious *Science* Quest…?"

"And sometimes science is used to help fight wars. Remember Archimedes in our Greek adventure?"

"That didn't end well for him!"[2]

"Science is part of our world, not cocooned from real events. Military commanders often make use of new developments in weapons and machines, as well as pay for research. What scientists decide to do with their discoveries influences everyone's lives. That's why ordinary people need to know what is going on and help scientists decide right from wrong."

Milton agrees with that, so sits back to listen. "OK, how did we get from Marie's laboratory to the desert?"

"Remember how Niels Bohr discovered the tightly packed nucleus of the atom?"

Milton nods. "You tricked me about the plum pudding though. Just as well we had bananas and sardines in the cupboard."

What's a nuclear scientist's favourite meal?

Fission chips!

---

2 If you want to find out about the curious death of Archimedes, see *Greek Adventure*, book 2 of our quest.

Harriet pats his back in apology. "Scientists realized that the nucleus was full of energy. Radioactive elements have a densely packed and unstable nucleus – a little like a balloon that can be popped. If you bombard the nucleus with particles, two results are possible. You can split the atom, releasing energy. This is called fission and is the kind of process used for electricity generation in most nuclear power plants. Aside from the damage of the bomb blast, one of the big effects is that it produces radioactive fallout that lasts for a very long time. People can get very ill and die from radioactivity long after the first explosion.

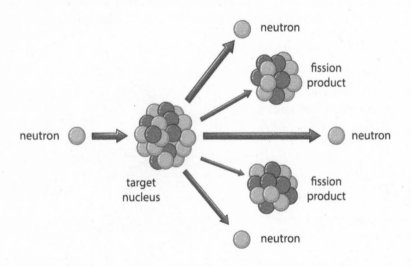

"The second way is when your particle is absorbed by the nucleus and turns the atom into a new element. This is called fusion because the atom and particle *fuse* together. It is the kind of reaction that goes on in the sun, where hydrogen fuses to form helium, releasing lots of energy. Without that, there would be no life on earth."

"Cool!" exclaims Milton.

"Yes, the world would be very cool indeed without fusion energy! Potentially the radioactive fallout is much less in this process – next to nothing in a perfect system – but it is very hard to achieve because you are trying to put a star like the sun in a box. Scientists are still working on how to do it as it would be a great source of energy and help us battle climate change. They know the theory but the engineering of the box is a real challenge!"

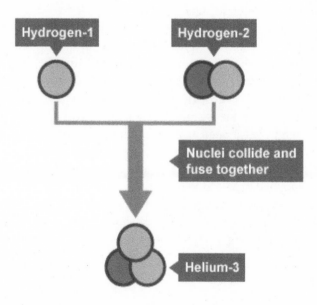

A countdown begins over a loudspeaker.

"Ladies and gentlemen, please put on your sunglasses," says the announcer.

Deep in the desert, the first nuclear bomb is ticking down to explosion.

"These people aren't making power for the electricity grid, are they?" whispers Milton. "They're using it to make bombs for fighting a war."

Harriet looks at him sadly. "And a terrible war it is too. I remember it well. Hitler, the leader of Germany, took over much of Europe and, with his ally, Japan, was threatening the world. Many European scientists of Jewish descent fled and ended up working with other scientists in what was called the Manhattan Project. Then they were faced with a terrible choice: they knew that Hitler's researchers were also working on nuclear weapons, so should they also? It was a race to get there first because they knew he'd use them for evil purposes. With that prospect to spur them on, they succeeded. This is the big question I told you about. If you have a terrible weapon like a bomb and know that your enemy might get it soon if the war carries on, do you use it to bring the battle to an end?"

"Um…" Milton isn't sure. He's also heard awful things about what happened in World War II.

The countdown reaches its conclusion: "Three… two… one!"

Out in the desert, a huge mushroom cloud rises up, with shockwaves rippling out from the centre of the explosion.

Harriet shakes her head sadly. "Or is the weapon so terrible that it should never be used under any circumstances? Hitler had been defeated by 1945 without it, but Japan was fighting on. Hundreds of thousands of people died at Hiroshima and Nagasaki when American planes dropped two bombs on Japan soon after this test. That did produce a quick end to the war but the human cost was huge. Most of the people who died weren't soldiers but ordinary men, women, and children."

"I don't know," says Milton. "That seems wrong but the Americans were in a bad situation fighting a desperate war. Did they have to drop it on people? Wouldn't proving they had it be enough?"

Harriet sighs. "I don't know, Milton. The scientists weren't the ones who decided where and how to drop it; that was the decision of the military and the political leaders. But I think it does show that scientific curiosity leads us into very difficult places, not just wonderful ones."

"So how do we know what we should do?"

"We mustn't forget that morality, or values of right and wrong, isn't going to be found in a test tube. You have to look beyond the laboratory for that in other kinds of knowledge."

"Where then?"

"I'd start in values built over the ages from philosophy and religion. Love for your neighbour, the duty to look after nature, and other teachings like that. Society – that means everyone – must always think of the rights and wrongs of how science is used. We now have weapons of mass destruction and these need to be in the very safest hands – or even better, removed by international agreement."

Milton is feeling very glum. "Harriet, these modern flights of scientific discovery are very upsetting. Can't we go on a happier adventure?"

Harriet shivers. "I agree. I've thought of something that you'll like. What would you say to a visit to Albert Einstein?"

"Oh yes!" Milton hurries back to the time machine. "I'm going to comb my fur in honour." Milton wriggles out of the hazmat suit and fluffs up his coat so he looks like a puff ball, rather like Einstein's hair in the famous photos of him.

Harriet chuckles, knowing Milton is doing this on purpose to cheer her up. "Right, then. Let's go back in time again to Bern in Switzerland in 1905."

"To a university?" Milton settles down to watch time and space fly by.

"No, to a street outside an office. The greatest scientist of the twentieth century started his celebrated career while doing an ordinary job as a clerk."

Einstein and the Tram

Our time travellers emerge from their box to find themselves on a street in Bern one evening in May 1905. They've landed in the shadow of a splendid medieval clock tower. It is a pleasant spring day and people are chatting and walking slowly home from work.

"Something big is about to happen," whispers Harriet. "After centuries of being the only system in town, the physics of Newton is about to be shaken to the core. All we need now is for Einstein to stop on his way home from his office."

"Where is he?" Milton is gazing at all the white-haired old men, looking for a familiar face.

"Milton, you're looking at the wrong people. He's only twenty-six in 1905."

"You mean that the scientist who overturned centuries of physics is *that* young?"

"Yes! Sometimes young thinkers, not bound by years of habit, can challenge ideas older people accept. Ah, there he is now!" Harriet hurries slowly towards a dark-haired young man running for the tram. "Oh no! Something's going wrong! If he catches that tram, he won't be here for the clock to strike – that isn't how this is supposed to go!"

"Leave it to me." Milton bounds over and gets tangled in the boots of the famous scientist. "Me-ow!" Einstein stumbles and Milton limps pitifully and makes big eyes up at young man.

Einstein stops. "I'm so sorry, Mr Cat, I didn't see you there." The doors to his tram close while Einstein checks over Milton's paws and tail. "Fortunately, you seem to be unhurt. Will you accept a stroke in apology?"

Milton purrs and preens under Einstein's hands. Harriet catches up.

"My word, someone's lost a tortoise." Einstein looks around but can see no pet owner. "What am I going to do with you?" He picks Harriet up and eyes her closely. "You look as though you've seen a few years. I wonder what stories you can tell about the past?"

Harriet is sorely tempted but she bites her tongue. She mustn't distract him, not when he should be making a great leap forward in his thinking.

Just then the crowd's murmuring stops as the statue of a cockerel on the clock crows, announcing that the timepiece is about to strike. It is a magnificent performance as the makers have included puppets of dancing bears, a knight on a white horse, a dancing jester, and the figure of Father Time opening his mouth with every toll of the bell.

Einstein laughs when the chiming ceases. "I always find that so amusing, no matter how often I see it. Time is a very interesting thing, don't you agree?" He looks down the iron track after his disappearing ride. Harriet holds her breath. Here it comes! "Imagine what would have happened if I'd got on that tram – and then the tram suddenly sped up to go at the speed of light. What would be the result?"

"He'd get home much quicker than he planned," hisses Milton.

Harriet gives him a withering look. The last thing they want is for Einstein to break his chain of thought.

"If I were sitting in my normal seat looking at my pocket watch," says Einstein, "it would carry on ticking in my hand. If I look back at the town clock though, while I'm travelling at the speed of light, the clock would appear to be at a standstill – no dancing jester, no Father Time opening his mouth. The clock would appear frozen in that moment. What does that mean?"

Harriet knows the answer – because Einstein himself has come up with it. She presses her jaws together.

"Hmm, I suppose it means," says Einstein slowly, "that time is relative to the person observing it. What an interesting idea. Newton never thought of that. I think I'd better do some more work on this." He puts Harriet down and takes out a notebook. While he is busy writing down his thoughts, Harriet and Milton slink away. He has too much thinking to do to worry about returning pets to their owners.

Back in the time machine, Harriet sighs happily. "Milton, you saved the day!"

Milton washes his paws modestly.

"You helped Einstein come up with the theory of special relativity. In it, he reconciles the equations that our friend James Clerk Maxwell devised for magnetism and electricity with the laws of mechanics.[3] He also comes up with his own equation. I think you know that one already."

---

3 Meet the amazing James Clerk Maxwell in *Victorian Voyages*, book 5 of our quest.

"Me?" Milton looks surprised. "I like maths but I'm not at Einstein's standard."

Harriet waves her front legs. "Tell me the one equation everyone knows."

Milton thinks hard and the answer comes to him. "$E=mc^2$?"

"Correct."

"I can say it but I don't know what the letters mean."

"In words, it means energy equals mass times the speed of light squared. Mass is the word scientists use to describe what feels to us like the weight of something."

$E = mc^2$

Energy equals mass times the speed of light squared.

MASS AND WEIGHT

Mass is not the same as weight. Mass is the amount of stuff (atoms) in an object. Weight is the result of a force working on that stuff; for example, Milton would be heavier standing on scales in earth's gravitation field than on the moon where the gravity is less strong.

"You don't need to follow the mathematics yet but it is good to understand that it comes from the new special relativity Einstein discovered in 1905. But he didn't stop there. He went on to a second big discovery: general relativity. Let's go and see that in action."

Trampoline universe

Milton is expecting to end up in another office or laboratory in the early twentieth century, but when he gets out of the time machine, he finds that Harriet has brought him to a trampoline park. From the clothes, they have landed close in time to the present day. Children are bouncing happily up and down, some doing somersaults, others jumping in pairs.

"Hey, Harriet, this looks fun!" Milton is itching to have a go.

"It's actually the best illustration of the theory of general relativity I could think of," says Harriet, pleased with her surprise. "Let's go to an empty trampoline."

Winding through the legs of the customers, they find one. They climb up to the edge and look at the smooth elastic surface spread out before them. It's very inviting, thinks Milton, pressing it lightly with his paw.

"Imagine what you're looking at is space–time," says Harriet.

"What's that?"

"It's our normal three dimensions of space fused with time. It's how we all experience the universe as physical beings moving in it and aging."

"Mmm, OK. Space–time is life as we know it. Got it."

"Now go into the centre of the trampoline."

"Can I bounce?"

"I'd prefer you to wait."

Milton gingerly steps across the stretchy surface and sits in the middle. He's not been holding back on the snacks recently so the material bulges beneath him.

"Now imagine yourself as a huge heavy object…"

"Hey!"

"Something the size of a star, or a black hole, which is a collapsed star."

"Oh, all right." Milton screws up his whiskers and pictures this. "Got it!"

"What have you done to space–time?"

Milton looks down at the trampoline. "I've bent it – just a little."

"Watch this." Harriet takes out a chocolate ball sweet and rolls it towards him. When it reaches the sagging trampoline, it curves towards Milton and ends up at his paws.

"Is this for me?"

"Not yet. Imagine that is a particle of light, a photon. What's happened to it?"

"It got caught in the space–time curve and very happily ended up right by my feet." He smiles hopefully at her.

"So your mass affected it long before it reached you?"

"Yes."

"That's general relativity – a theory about gravitation. It's how we came to understand about black holes, objects in the universe with such high gravitational pull that not even light can escape."

"So I'm a black hole now? A hungry one?" Milton licks his lips.

"Oh, go on. And you can bounce too."

TRY THIS AT HOME: BUILD YOUR OWN MODEL OF SPACE-TIME AND GENERAL RELATIVITY

You can try this for yourself. You need a trampoline (hopefully someone you know will have one in their garden), a few friends to be planets, and some spherical sweets (marbles will work too but are less fun because you can't eat them!).

Start by asking one friend to get into the centre. Note what happens to the surface of space–time (otherwise known as the trampoline!). Then roll your photons (sweets) towards her. What happens?

Next ask another friend to join her and repeat. What happens when you have double the mass in the middle?

Carry on until you run out of friends (or sweets!). And if an adult asks what you are doing, you can explain Einstein's theory of general relativity to them and they will be very impressed!

Harriet sits back and enjoys watching Milton's acrobatics. If he is a black hole, he's like none she's ever seen from the time machine before, apart from consuming everything that comes too near him. After half an hour, she checks her watch.

"Milton, time to go. We are going to watch another of Einstein's predictions being proved."

Feeling a little dizzy, Milton makes his way back to her. "Oh? Are we going back to his time?"

"That's not necessary. Some of his ideas were proved during his lifetime – for example, that the sun's gravity would bend light from other stars. That was shown by Sir Arthur Eddington during a solar eclipse in 1919. Eddington travelled to an island off Africa where he could view a long total eclipse and make the measurements. He showed that Einstein was correct. That idea could be proven by the equipment available at the time, but other ones needed very special kit and had to wait.

LIGHT BENDING DURING ECLIPSE

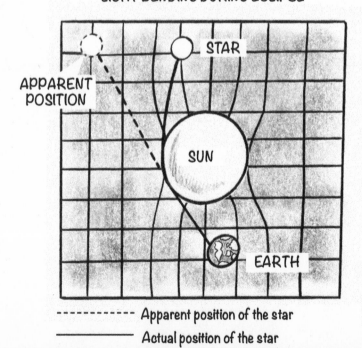

--------- Apparent position of the star
―――――― Actual position of the star

"One of Einstein's predictions was only shown to be true a hundred years later when the equipment was up to the job of detecting the event he described."

"That's a long time," agrees Milton.

"And it shows how the big picture scientists create sometimes goes a little ahead of the evidence and then has to wait to be tested. It is very wrong to think of scientists as limited to known facts; the greatest ones are some of the most imaginative people I've met, making leaps to a new big picture when they can't quite justify why they think they might be right."

At times I feel certain I am right while not knowing the reason...

Imagination is more important than knowledge.

For knowledge is limited, whereas imagination embraces the entire world...

It is, strictly speaking, a real factor in scientific research.

"So are you taking me to meet some more imaginative people?" asks Milton.

"They certainly have awe-inspiring ambition, running a really big expensive experiment with no certainty that it would give them the results they wanted."

"How big?"

"The width of the United States of America – and to the beginnings of the universe."

"That's pretty big," agrees Milton.

"We're not going far from the trampoline park to the LIGO Hanford Observatory in Washington State – that's in the north-west of the country," continues Harriet. "It's 2015 so watch out for traffic on the roads."

Milton is not paying attention. "Did you say Lego?"

"No, LIGO. It stands for Laser Interferometer Gravitational-Wave Observatory."

"Ooh, big words."

"It means they are watching for gravitational waves. If Einstein's theory is correct, the collision of two large bodies will produce them."

Just as they reach the exit from the park, Milton watches two big children bounce into each other and knock heads. The result is that both end up in floods of tears, calling for their parents.

"Collisions like that?"

Harriet chuckles. Neither child is hurt and they are soon comforted. "It's a picture, I suppose, but their reaction only lasted a few seconds and was very noisy. These gravitational waves have been travelling through the universe for over a billion years and are so tiny that they are extremely hard to detect on earth."

After a brisk walk, the two time travellers enter the LIGO control room. Behind the rows of computer screens are many excited scientists.

"They've been working on this for years," whispers Harriet. "There are two LIGO sites – the other is on the opposite side of America in the south-east. People from all over the world have been involved in the project. The theory is that gravitational waves from the collision of two huge black holes long ago might be detectable in the observatories as a tiny gravitational ripple."

New data flashes up on the biggest screen and the scientists erupt into applause, cheers, and tears.

"Something just happened?" asks Milton.

"Oh yes," says one woman, wiping away tears of joy and hugging him. "We've detected a change in our equipment a thousandth of the width of a proton!" Clearly this is good news.

43

"Oh – um, well done," says Milton, patting her shoulder and purring.

The astronomer is so happy, she doesn't even stop to consider she is talking to a cat. Champagne corks pop and the scientists go into party mode. Milton squirms free from the woman before she remembers it was a cat who congratulated her.

"See how exciting being a scientist can be?" asks Harriet. "It's lots of hard work, but like detectives following clues, you get rewarded with seeing the mystery solved and the universe comes that little more into focus."

"And you have parties," says Milton, snagging a bag of crisps and a party popper. He watches the celebrations around him thoughtfully. Science has changed so much – at least, the kind of people following it as a career has changed since the beginning of the twentieth century. There are women and men from all nations gathered in the room. He wonders what kind of ideas inspire them on their quest. He decides to ask Harriet.

"The other great physicists we've met on our quest – Newton, Faraday, and Maxwell – have all been people with a belief in God," Milton begins. "But it was Einstein's ideas that brought all these people here today. What did he believe, other than in the power of the imagination? Did God fit into his big picture of the universe like it did for Maxwell?"

Harriet sneaks a mouthful of lettuce from a tray of sandwiches laid out for the party. "That's a very interesting question. Einstein came from a Jewish background, which is why he left Europe in 1933. Hitler's brutal government was persecuting Jewish people, eventually killing millions in the Holocaust. Einstein took shelter in America.

"As for his own faith, he didn't believe in a personal God who answers prayer, but did believe that the most mysterious thing about the universe was that we could understand it, and that the laws of nature showed the existence of what he called 'a spirit vastly superior to that of man', which should make us humble.

Awe and wonder, he once said, were 'the sower of all true science', by which he meant they planted the seeds in us that grew into curiosity about the world."

Gravitation cannot be held responsible for people falling in love.

"I like the sound of him," says Milton. "I feel humble too when I look up at the universe, even if I'm not sure about what lies behind it – so I can understand that."

"Being humble and open-minded is a good quality in a scientist," agrees Harriet. "If you remember the people we've met, we've found that quality in scientists from all kinds of faiths and no faith. I think the key is not believing you already know everything, and being willing if necessary to challenge the old big picture. If Einstein hadn't been able to imagine new ideas about gravity, maybe we'd never have had his theories, which went on to reshape physics."

Leaving the party still going on, they stroll back through the evening shadows to where they left their time machine.

The strange world of quantum physics

Einstein has given them a lot to think about. Milton has been reading up on physics while Harriet has had a nap. He can hear her stirring, and her head pops out of her shell with a yawn.

"Hello, sleepyhead! Ready for our next adventure?" he asks.

"After breakfast, yes, I will be." She munches on a dandelion picked at the trampoline park.

"So where do you want to go today?" asks Milton.

Breakfast over, Harriet settles into her favourite armchair by the porthole and gets out her knitting. "Actually, this is your moment to be in charge of the next stage of our quest. How have you got on with your reading on quantum physics?"

Milton pats the pile of journals and books he's been studying. "Good. It's been especially interesting as it involves my owner,

Erwin Schrödinger. I'm not sure I realized when he gave me my dish of food each day how clever he was. I thought he was here to brush and feed me."

Harriet chuckles. "I imagine he was able to multitask. You now know more about this area of science than me. I've always been a bit confused by it."

"You mean quantum physics?" Milton pirouettes with excitement. "You're right. I might not know as much about the history of science as you, Harriet, but I do know lots of exciting things now about atoms. For example, I know what questions quantum science is asking today."

"Then you can choose our destination." She knits a row on her scarf, keeping half an eye on him as he is still learning how to fly the machine.

Milton goes to the control desk and thinks. It is harder than he imagined. There are so many possibilities.

"Milton, you aren't by any chance being uncertain, are you?" teases Harriet, adding a new colour to her knitting project.

Milton grins as inspiration strikes. "If I am, that's the best introduction to quantum physics. It is a very weird world and has made me into a very uncertain cat. Give me a moment and I'll give you a list of the odd things that happen at the very smallest, or quantum, level." He quickly draws up a list, using his tail as a brush to add some illustrations.

MILTON'S SUPER–STRANGE WORLD OF QUANTUM PHYSICS

Quantum physics started with the discovery that energy comes in tiny packets at the atomic scale, unlike the earlier physics of bigger things. It leads to ideas that seem at first glance to go against everything we expect to see – but they really do exist. Here are some examples:

• **Particle-wave duality**: tiny subatomic things like electrons can either be particles or waves, depending on how you look at them. ("Subatomic" means the things that make up atoms – proton, neutron, electron, etc.) Specialized experiments can even make this duality work with larger things like molecules.

Is it a particle? Is it a wave? Neither by itself. It's a quantum! You need more mathematics than even Milton knows to be able to see how a quantum can be both a particle and a wave.

• **Quantum tunnelling**: this is when particles pass through barriers that classical physics say they can't. Here's a picture to explain. You're bouncing the ball against a wall. It bounces back and you catch it. You repeat. Then one time you throw it, the ball disappears from your side of the wall and appears on the other and carries on travelling. It hasn't passed over the wall, just gone through it to the other side without making a hole!

Very strange? But it's also the reason we're alive. As we saw, the sun works on nuclear fusion. The process that produces the fused atoms relies on quantum tunnelling, so without it we would be very much left in the dark!

- **Superposition**: at the quantum level, particles are able to do opposite things at the same time. To picture this, imagine being able to spin in two directions at once! Not even the best acrobat can do that.

Super strange? It is, but if you or someone you know ever goes in a MRI machine in a hospital to have a scan of the brain or another part of the body, the machine does this to the hydrogen protons in the body – and when they decay to a definite single direction, a picture can be built up of what's going on inside.

- **Entanglement**: this is quantum at its most weird. Albert Einstein called it 'spooky action at a distance'. Through entanglement, if you have two objects that no longer have any interaction with each other, measurements of them relate to each other in a remarkable way.

    Suppose you have a pair of gloves, and you post one glove to one friend and the other to another friend. If one of them receives a left glove then they know immediately that the other friend has received a right glove, even without phoning each other. Entanglement is a bit like that, only even weirder and more surprising.

Everything, including us, is made up of quantum stuff – and understanding the quantum world helps run computers, nuclear power stations, lasers, and even a smartphone. Just imagine – when we switch on our phones each day, we are calling on the super-strange world of quantum physics!

Harriet has got her knitting in a tangle while reading about this.

Milton helps her unpick the knots.

"Oh Milton, I'm feeling too old to get my mind around this," she admits. "And I don't have a smartphone."

"You don't need one. You are smart enough on your own and you have a time machine." Milton pats her shoulder. He is used to Harriet taking everything in her slow stride, but he knows that many people are frightened off by the strange things they've heard about quantum physics. "I think the pictures used to describe the quantum world are hard to grasp because our minds can't go against what we are used to. We only see things spin in one direction, be in one place at a time, and so on."

Harriet resolves to try to understand this world as best she can. It is clearly very important to the future of science. "So how do they know enough to be able to use it to make complicated machines like body scanners?"

"That's because they do have an accurate description of how the quantum level works – one that can be used in experiments and technology."

"What kind of description?"

"My favourite sort – mathematical! My maths isn't up to it yet but I've been told that equations describe these things very well."

Harriet tries to imagine this. She is coming to terms with things being able to spin in two directions. But going through the wall…

Seeing her pained expression, Milton smiles. "You're in good company, Harriet. You aren't alone in finding it hard: Einstein also struggled. He didn't like the uncertainties in the quantum system. Would it help to see how we got from Einstein to those strange phenomena I described?"

God does not play dice.

"Yes, I think so."

"I'll show you in simple steps I've noted down from my reading."

MILTON'S SIMPLE STEPS TO QUANTUM

• In 1900, the German scientist Max Planck was looking at radiation in the laboratory. He realized there were separate packets – quanta – of energy and that these came in the same amount for a given wavelength of light.

Science cannot solve the ultimate mystery of nature. And that is because... we ourselves are a part of the mystery that we are trying to solve.

• In the 1920s, my master, Erwin Schrödinger, used a special kind of maths to calculate finding an electron in a certain position. He showed that maths could help you see into this very small world.

• In 1927, his friend Werner Heisenberg came up with what is called the "uncertainty principle". This states that there are limits to what we can know. For example, the more you know about the position of a particle, the less you can know about the momentum and vice versa...

Harriet puts the paper down. "This sounds a bit like our Greek friend Zeno's paradox about the arrow in flight. That's where we learned about paradoxes, all those thousands of years ago."[4]

"That's right. The reason why we all find quantum hard to imagine is because it is full of paradoxes that Zeno would've loved. He probably would've been a quantum physicist if he were alive today."

"Without a doubt," agrees Harriet, and goes back to reading.

• Heisenberg's uncertainty principle led to the famous thought experiment named after me, Schrödinger's Cat. (I have to stress NO real cats were used in this experiment as my master is a cat lover and WOULD NEVER do that.) He imagined that a cat is in a box with a bottle of deadly poison and a radioactive device that triggers the release of the poison if one atom decays. It may or may not do so – we don't know. The idea is that in the quantum world there is something called "superposition" – two states can exist at the same time, like looking at two pictures layered or superimposed on top of each other. The cat is alive *and* dead – until we look. Then we find out if he has survived. In fact, our looking triggers the outcome by making a measurement. Make sense? Not really, and that was why my master came up with it to challenge the Heisenberg model. Scientists are still arguing about it.

---

4 You can meet Zeno in *Greek Adventure*.

- The English scientist Paul Dirac worked out in the 1930s that to balance what we know at the quantum level, there must be antimatter to the matter we observe. He called his particle a "positron", the antiparticle of electron. Lots of other antimatter particles have also been discovered.

SCHRODINGER'S CAT

WANTED

DEAD AND ALIVE

The greatest experiment on earth!

The time machine lands. Harriet checks the time and finds that it is 2012. Outside she can see distant snow-capped mountains. She recognizes the big lake that lies at their foot.

"I think I can guess where you've brought me," she says. "The Large Hadron Collider near Geneva in Switzerland."

"Is it a good surprise?" asks Milton. He's a little nervous as he's not been in charge before – not since Harriet was tortoise-napped over a thousand years ago.

"Oh yes, I've always wanted to see it."

"It's impressive, isn't it? The largest machine on earth – and its tunnel runs in a ring for 27 kilometres (16⅓ miles) under both Switzerland and France, so even that makes it unique." Milton opens the door and they step out into the car park at CERN, the European Organization for Nuclear Research.

"I've heard they are trying to recreate the start of the universe, or Big Bang. Is it safe to be here?" asks Harriet.

"Very safe. The machine is buried 100 metres underground. The only casualty so far has been a stone marten, a little weasel creature, that got inside and gnawed through a cable. It was electrocuted and broke the machine too, so they won't let that happen again. Health and safety rules!"

They enter the building and travel down in an elevator to the level from which the scientists watch the experiments on their computer screens. Harriet marvels at how far physics has travelled – from one man looking at a Swiss town clock to huge machines run by teams of women and men under the countryside.

"What are they doing with their tunnel ring?" asks Harriet.

Milton licks his paws, beginning to enjoy being the leader on this part of the quest. He smooths down his fur, which is still a little fluffy after his Einstein episode. "Remember where you left us with the atom? They had just learned to split it and release energy."

"Oh yes."

"This means that physicists realized that the atom wasn't the fundamental, or smallest, part of the building blocks of life. We have protons, neutrons, and electrons and so on inside the atom."

"That's right."

"They then found that even they weren't the foundation. You could go smaller still, to the little bits, or quarks, that make up a proton and neutron. And they are still discovering more of these little particles, so the story might not yet be finished."

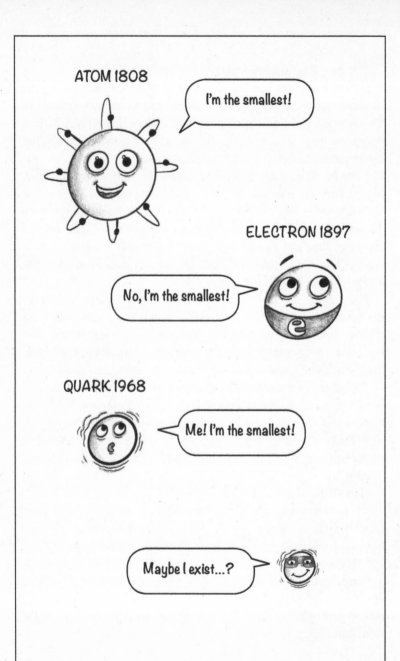

The scientists gather around their monitors as the accelerator hums into action.

"They usually find the particles by working out that there is a gap in what they observe versus what the mathematics suggests exists. Maths is so cool that it often gets there first." Milton helps Harriet into a good spot to watch what's going on. "The scientists get the hint and go on to look for the particles. That's why they built the Large Hadron Collider. Among others exploring these questions were three scientists: Robert Brout, François Englert, and Peter Higgs. They were thinking about the problem in the standard model of physics: how to explain mass, which is related to weight. Why are some particles heavy and others have no mass at all? They thought it might be because particles interact via something they called the Brout–Englert–Higgs mechanism with a field, which they called the Higgs field."

"They named all this after themselves?"

Milton grins and licks his paws. "Wouldn't you? Another reason to go into science – you could get cool stuff named after you! Anyway, the machine looks for something called the Higgs boson, a special particle that might be detected if the protons in the accelerator smash into each other at high speed."

"How fast is fast?"

"Close to the speed of light."

Harriet sits down. Thinking of crashing at this speed makes her feel dizzy.

Milton is getting carried away. He loves everything about this branch of science. "Deep in this tunnel, particle beams are running in rings, directed on their way by powerful super-cooled magnets. The magnets steer the beam without friction so the particles can go very fast. It's a bit like when sliding on ice compared to sliding on a pavement."

Harriet hasn't slid on ice ever, not even as a young tortoise, but decides not to mention this as Milton is in full flow.

"And I think... yes..." says Milton, his whiskers pricking up.

The scientists erupt in cheers.

"What's just happened?" ask Harriet.

"They detected a Higgs boson – which means the Higgs field exists – which means physicists might be able to go on to explain mass."

"Is that the only thing they're doing here, explaining mass?"

"Oh no, the accelerator is useful for testing lots of other cutting-edge theories. For example, they are also looking for dark matter and dark energy."

"They sound exciting."

"If we can find them, they will be. It is a bit of a head-scratcher that the stars and planets in the universe only make up 4 per cent of the matter we think exists. Where's the rest of it? That's why it is called dark matter."

Harriet flops down on the nearest couch. "It is one very strange universe we live in."

"And it might not be the only one there is. One of the ways to explain the maths suggests that the sums work if you allow there to be lots of universes, or multiverses."

If the universe is one of many multiverses...

Harriet has heard of this too. "Thanks to what is happening at the smallest level of quantum, the big picture has got very, very big, hasn't it? It's hard to hold on to our own place when we think of all these new discoveries of the very small and the extremely huge."

Milton curls up beside her and purrs to comfort her. "But without us to be curious about them, what would be the point? Have you ever thought of that?"

"I am thinking about it now. We are needed to investigate it, aren't we, or none of this would be known to anyone?"

"And here's an exciting thought: maybe the universe is set on a course to become self-aware – which is what we are when we are curious. That's what some scientists think. And even the ones who believe it has no point and is random – and that our self-awareness is just a quirk of our brains – still ask questions. They want to find out more, even if they don't have an answer for why they do it."

"It's all very, very curious," sighs Harriet.

Milton purrs. "On that everyone agrees!"

WHERE NEXT FOR EVOLUTION?

"We've gone a very long way with physics so far in our modern flight," says Harriet. "Are you ready to go back to biology?"

"Yes, please. And you'd better take back control as that's your area more than mine." Milton washes his paws and rubs his face.

"Thank you. I thought you made a splendid team leader. So shall we find out what happened to Darwin's Theory of Evolution?" asks Harriet.[5]

Pausing in his cleaning routine, Milton thinks back. "I enjoyed that adventure. I met the younger you!"

"And you saved the universe."

"I'm glad you remember that." Milton polishes his claws.

"We left scientists in the nineteenth century looking for a way that characteristics could be passed down between parent and child – it was the missing piece of the puzzle in the new big picture that life evolved over long periods of time."

"Sounds good. I like puzzles!" says Milton. "Where does that take us?"

"Hmm." Harriet ponders her choices. "Have a look at this little note I've prepared while I decide."

---

5   To accompany Darwin on his evolutionary adventure, go to *Victorian Voyages*.

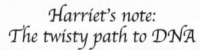

Harriet's note:
The twisty path to DNA

People often say that DNA was discovered by the British scientist Francis Crick (1916–2004) and his American colleague James Watson (1928–) but that is not true – they discovered its *structure*.[6] DNA itself had been found much earlier and it truly was an international effort.

•   Yucky start – 1860s: A Swiss chemist, Johannes Friedrich Miescher, finds a substance he calls "nuclein" from pus on hospital bandages.

•   Pairing up – 1878: The German anatomist (someone who studies the way bodies are structured) Walther Flemming publishes his findings on the fibre-like structures in the nuclei of cells – these come to be called **chromosomes.**

•   Building a strong base – 1881: The German biochemist Albrecht Kossel discovers the five bases, or building blocks, of "nuclein" and gives it the name of **DNA**.

•   Peas to meet you again – early 1900s: The work on inheritance in peas by Gregor Mendel, an Austrian scientist and abbot of a monastery in Brno, is rediscovered. Scientists begin to realize its significance.[7]

•   Two paths leading to same destination – also early 1900s: The American biologist Walter Sutton and Theodor Boveri, a German, both come up with the idea that **genetic** material is passed from parent to child in chromosomes.

---

6 For more about the role of deoxyribonucleic acid or DNA and chromosomes in evolution see *Cave Discovery*, book 1 of our quest.

7 You can find out more about Mendel in *Victorian Voyages*!

- Biochemists provide the Lego bricks – around 1910: The Russian Phoebus Levene works out the order of three major components in DNA, and, in 1950, the Austrian Erwin Chargaff discovers that DNA keeps certain properties the same even in different species. Sound complicated? Imagine it as being given a fixed number of differently coloured but same-shaped Lego to build a tower. The model of DNA is going to take shape in a limited number of ways.

After that, things speed up in the early 1950s…!
- X-ray vision – Two English scientists, Rosalind Franklin and Maurice Wilkins, take remarkable X-ray crystallography images of DNA.
- 3D modelling – The American scientist Linus Pauling is making progress on his three-dimensional structures. He's getting very close but…
- Double down – 1953: Watson and Crick publish their finding that DNA has a double helix structure joined by hydrogen bonds – like two hydrogen atoms holding hands across the twisting model.

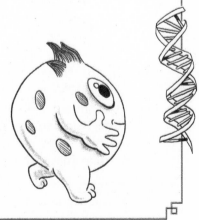

Milton puts down the paper. "So are we going to see Crick and Watson discover the structure?"

Harriet's paw hovers over the controls. "That would mean a trip to Cambridge, or to King's College London, where Franklin and Wilkins are taking their X-rays. It is an exciting race, and not without arguments as everyone is very competitive to get to the finish first. Watson, Crick, and Wilkins all go on to receive the Nobel Prize."

Milton is suspicious. "Why not Rosalind Franklin? Was it because she is a woman?"

"No. Sadly Rosalind Franklin dies before she can be nominated.[8] But it is true that her part is downplayed for decades after her death because many male scientists still weren't used to the idea of the women in the laboratory being their equal. It could be a bit of a boys' club at this time."

THE MYSTERY OF PHOTOGRAPH 51

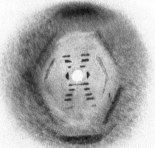

One of the famous rows about the discovery of the structure of DNA is Franklin's Photograph 51. One story goes that she was making fast progress to unravelling the structure, thanks to her images, but her colleague Wilkins showed the images, particularly number 51, to the visitors Watson and Crick without her permission.

---

8 The Nobel Prize isn't given to people after their death.

However, another version goes that the image belonged to the university so he could do this without asking, and she would've been happy to take part in such scientific collaboration anyway. It just goes to show that the picture of truth can get very blurred even when within living memory!

"So we're not going there?" asks Milton.

"I think not. We've been to London and Cambridge quite a few times on our travels." Harriet smiles at him over the top of the control desk. "Let's go somewhere much closer to our day and unravel the human genome! That means a flight back to America."

TRY THIS AT HOME: EXTRACT DNA FROM A STRAWBERRY

You don't have to go to a forensic laboratory to see DNA – you can extract it at home yourself. For this experiment there is one step that requires an adult to help, but most of it is surprisingly super-easy! You will need:

1 strawberry
1 plastic sandwich bag
2 teaspoons washing-up liquid
½ teaspoon salt
Coffee filter paper
Clear plastic beaker
Some water
Rubbing alcohol or surgical spirit (with adult help)

Now follow these simple steps:
- Put the strawberry in the bag and gently mash it up to a pulp.
- Add the salt, washing-up liquid, and half a cup of water.
- Seal the bag and mix gently. Try not to create bubbles!
- Now pour through a coffee filter paper into a plastic beaker below. Be gentle – you don't want the filter paper to split!
- You now have the DNA in the beaker, but it is in solution. You need to do a process called "precipitation" – turning it back to something solid. Ask an adult to pour the surgical spirit into the beaker to double the volume.
- Watch what happens. Can you see the solution separating? The slimy stuff gathering at the top is strawberry DNA. You can now use a lollipop stick to lift it out and have a look.
- You can watch top scientists doing this experiment here: https://www.youtube.com/watch?v=hOpu4iN5Bh4

Human genome – our instruction book

Harriet and Milton arrive in a big auditorium. News teams are gathered from all over the world and there is an excited buzz in the air. Milton and Harriet find it very easy to slip in at the back unnoticed because everyone is looking at the stage.

"When are we?" whispers Milton.

"The year 2000."

"Some big event must have happened. Is there an election? It has to be something very important to bring all these journalists here."

"Science is about to make big news. That man in the middle is President Bill Clinton. His presence here shows that, unlike some we've visited back in history, these scientists are supported by the top people in power. In fact, one big change in our picture of science is that all modern nations think asking scientific questions is a good thing and they often contribute to research costs."

A camera operator almost steps on Milton's paws.

"Me-ow!" He leaps up to a good vantage point on a ledge to get clear. Harriet follows slowly, showing that some tortoises can climb walls too if given enough time.

"Who else is here?" Milton asks when she arrives five minutes later.

"Next to the president is Craig Venter, a biologist, and the other man who is about to speak is Francis Collins. He's been leading the Human Genome Project as its director. This isn't the work of just two men, but lots of researchers. Another big change in science is that it is rarely now the work of one person on their own."

"What did you call it? The Gnome Project?" Milton is distracted by seeing one reporter open a bag of peanuts.

"No, *genome*. That means sequencing, or describing, all the genes in human DNA. Pay attention, Milton: history is about to be made!"

Milton tears his gaze from the nuts. Francis Collins has come to the microphone and announces that they have made a working draft of the human genome.

"It is humbling for me," says Collins, "and awe-inspiring to realize that we have caught the first glimpse of our own instruction book, previously known only to God."

His speech is met with huge applause.

"That's interesting," says Milton as the clapping dies away and the questions start. "Director Collins has mentioned God. I didn't think modern scientists would talk about religion in such a big announcement."

"That's because for Collins, his religious beliefs are now part of his motive for asking big questions. He started life as an atheist, read the works of another famous scholar called C. S. Lewis…"

"I know him!" says Milton excitedly. "Narnia, White Witch, Aslan! But he wasn't a scientist."

"Not all wisdom comes from the laboratory. Most scientists listen to other people, poets and writers, philosophers and theologians, too. There are different kinds of knowledge and the big picture can't be complete without them, as we'll see."

"All right. I understand that. We saw in 1945 that we needed other ways of deciding if using nuclear weapons was right or wrong. So what did Collins learn?"

"He was convinced out of his atheism by Lewis's argument about morality."

"You'll have to explain that." Milton settles down, head resting on his tail.

Harriet searches for an example. "Hmm. I know. If you saw me drowning in a river, would you try to save me?"

"Of course!"

"But that's against what evolution by natural selection would suggest – let the weak old tortoise drown and save yourself."

"But you're my friend. I'd probably even try to save a stranger if I could."

Harriet smiles. "Exactly! That is what led Collins to look for the spiritual nature of being a human, how such things are written on our hearts. He went from there to being a Christian.

"But the big picture of science is big enough to contain people with very different views. Other scientists, for example his colleague Craig Venter, who is standing next to him for this announcement, wouldn't use those words as he has a different motivation that doesn't include God. Science is, or should be, open to people from all backgrounds, religious and non-religious. Everyone sharing their curiosity is what is important for work in the laboratory."

Milton finds this new idea a challenge. "So how does that work? Haven't we seen that people have been falling out for centuries when religion and science get tangled up?"

"When science hasn't been travelling happily in the slipstream of the ultimate questions of faith and philosophy, yes, occasionally they have."

The God of the Bible is also the God of the genome. He can be worshipped in the cathedral or in the laboratory.

"But Director Collins is talking about it here!"

"That doesn't mean religion has no place in other settings, like in this announcement. It is just that you risk a crash if you try to use it to replace what you do in the laboratory, shaping what you find to fit some preconceived world view. In fact, a lot of people, like Director Collins, find it works the other way around for them. For many researchers, what they find in science increases their respect for the wonders of nature. Their world view adjusts to take in the new facts. For some that is a religious experience."

Milton suddenly remembers something Collins said. "He described their work as a draft. What does that mean?"

"That the complete book of the genome isn't quite ready; they need to check it over. They do so and finish it in 2003, on the fiftieth anniversary of the year Watson and Crick discovered the structure of DNA."

"And what do they do with the book? Is it an exciting read?"

Harriet chuckles. "Only to an expert. It is written in a string of repeating letters – A, C, G, T – which stand for the four different bases, or Lego bricks, that make up DNA. But here is how Director Collins describes it."

It's a history book – a narrative of the journey of our species through time. It's a shop manual, with an incredibly detailed blueprint for building every human cell.

And it's a transformative textbook of medicine, with insights that will give health care providers immense new powers to treat, prevent, and cure disease.

When Harriet turns around, she finds Milton flat on his back, paws in the air.

"Wow! I think this might be the most curious thing you've ever shown me," he says.

"Just wait," says Harriet. "There's a lot more to come. I'm taking you on your next adventure in evolution. Let's get back to the time machine."

LIVE LONG AND PROSPER!

While Harriet and Milton are travelling, it is a good opportunity to check in on the many advances in modern science. Life expectancy in richer countries over the last century has risen to 76 for men and 82 for women (a hundred years ago it was around 55 and 58). What's changed? Immunizations (jabs) for children are one big factor, as well as better health care for the elderly. But there's one big advance well worth knowing that's revolutionized how we fight disease: antibiotics!

MEET THE SCIENTIST

SIR ALEXANDER FLEMING

- Lived: 1881–1955
- Number of jobs: 2 (doctor and researcher into bacteria)
- Influence (out of 100): 99 (many of us are alive today thanks to his discovery of penicillin, the first antibiotic. Antibiotics fight bacteria, the germs that can make disease or wounds fatal. He opened a whole new area of medicine)
- Right? (out of 20): 20 (he showed how even accidental discoveries only produce a result if the observer is curious to find the cause. He already knew from his work as a doctor in World War I that more soldiers died of infection than disease or injuries, so the idea to find something to fight bacteria was already on his agenda. However, the actual discovery was a wonderful chance. He was a messy man. Coming back from holiday in 1928 he found his samples of the staphylococci bacteria had grown a mould. Most

of us would say "yuck!" and chuck them out, but not Dr Fleming. He noticed the mould was eating away at the bacteria – that mould was penicillin. His discovery at first was little noticed by his colleagues, and he had trouble working out a way to make it into a medicine, but antibiotics were on the way)

- Helpfully wrong? (out of 10): 8 (after a few years, he gave up trying to produce a form for medicine, thinking it too difficult, but he did hand over the work to two other researchers who went on to succeed. With government money behind them and a war to win, Howard Florey and Ernst Boris Chain in Oxford went on to find the answer to making penicillin into a medicine – and by the end of World War II there was enough penicillin to treat all Allied troops, saving huge numbers of lives)

- Interesting fact: one of the reasons he went into research at the beginning of his career at St Mary's Hospital was that the captain of his rifle club wanted to keep him on the team. He suggested this branch of study so his crack marksman could stay in London. It was a good thing for all of us that Dr Fleming's aim was so good, or maybe he wouldn't have stayed and gone into medical research.

WARNING

Antibiotics are the wonder medicine of the last century but we now have a BIG problem. They've proved so successful and are now so easily obtained that they've been overused both in humans and farm animals. If you don't handle them properly, the bacteria learn to fight back and the antibiotic no longer works. The medical experts are now trying to persuade everyone to be much more careful about what and how much we use or we will lose our best weapon in the fight against disease.

Evolution and the octopus

After a brief journey across time and space, Milton sniffs the air as he gets out of the time machine.

"We are in our time, aren't we, Harriet? Right up to date?"

Harriet follows him more slowly. They've journeyed so far together, and time travelling is hard work when you are as old as she is. "How do you know that, Milton?"

"I can smell fizzy drinks, petrol engines, and popcorn..."

"That doesn't narrow it down to our time – that could be any time in the last fifty years. What else?"

"Everyone is glued to their smartphones! Proof positive. They weren't doing that even in the year 2000!"

Harriet has to agree. People have adapted to the new devices and that has brought about a change in their behaviour.

"Welcome to the most recent stage in human evolution – the pod-estrian!" quips Milton in his best TV-announcer voice. He has to move quickly or be stepped on by people who aren't looking where they are going.

"At least it means they don't notice the time machine popping into existence in front of them. I've engaged the anti-image mode so we won't be visible to all the cameras in our time," says Harriet.

Milton has carried on sniffing while she is switching on the safety measures. "You know, Harriet, I can also smell fish! Yum!"

She chuckles and points up to the sign above their head. "These aren't for eating."

"It's in Chinese," says Milton.

"And it says 'Welcome to Shanghai's Ocean Aquarium Park'. It is one of the largest in the world with the longest underwater tunnel. I've brought you here because it is a good place to see octopuses, but you can see them in many aquaria around the world."

"Shouldn't that be octopi?" asks Milton, happy to get one over on clever old Harriet.

"I'm afraid not. The word is from Greek – so the plural would be 'octopodes' – but no one uses that in English."

"Then I'll stick with octopuses."

How do you remember what to call more than one octopus?

❌ octopi   ✓ octopuses

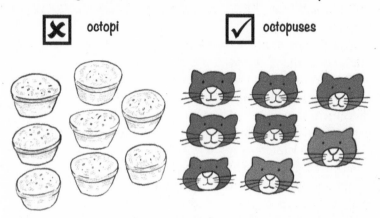

They scamper in under the cover of an excited school party. There is so much to see, but Harriet is on a mission to reach the display of octopuses.

"Slow down, Harriet!" This might be the first time anyone has ever said that to a tortoise, but Milton is getting very hungry seeing his favourite food swimming about just out of reach. "I like fish!" He approaches the glass but –

"Aargh!" squawks Milton.

A shark swims straight at him. His fur sticks out on end in alarm but the shark turns away just before it reaches the glass.

"Do you still like all fish?" asks Harriet. "Whale sharks are the biggest of the fish."

"Maybe not all fish – especially not those that eat me, rather than me eat them," agrees Milton.

They arrive in front of the tank for the octopuses.

"The name means 'eight' and 'foot' in Greek," explains Harriet, "because it famously has that number of tentacles. But I have a particular reason for bringing you eye to eye with this one."

"That's very interesting," says Milton. "Why?" He has entered a staring competition with the biggest specimen.

"Because we have reached the frontier of where ideas about evolution have got in our time. By now biologists agree that the outline of Darwin's Theory of Evolution is basically correct. We saw Mendel find the evidence that characteristics are inherited in recessive and dominant traits. We then went on to see Crick, Watson, Wilkins, and Franklin uncover DNA. Then scientists unravelled the genome of humans and made a start on other species. So we have the theory and the means, but how does evolution by natural selection work out in practice?"

Milton is taken aback by the question. He almost blinks but stops himself just in time. "You're asking me how I would test this?"

"Yes, Milton. You've travelled the whole history of science. I'm sure you have some good ideas."

"Well, I think I'd look out for the longest running experiment."

"Which is?"

"Life on earth!"

"Exactly. And when you look at that, you see many curious things. Biologists don't completely agree on the way evolution unfolds. A scientist called Stephen Jay Gould emphasized the randomness of evolution – which means that things change in no predictable way. In this model, if we reran the experiment of life on earth, we'd come up with something completely different."

Milton is still eye to eye with the octopus and wondering

where Harriet is going with this. "OK, I understand that. If by chance the human evolutionary ancestor gets squashed by a meteor or eaten by a predator, and that species doesn't survive, something completely different would've evolved in the place of humans."

"Correct. But others, like the biologist Simon Conway Morris, think that there is something called convergence, which means that if you reran the experiment you'd get an outcome very like the world we see today. He even says that this will likely hold true for life on other planets. So if aliens land they might well be bipedal – two-legged – with hands and a brain not unlike humans."

"Personally, I think they'll be four-legged and have a tail."

"And I think a shell pretty useful. But he is only having fun speculating when he says that. The point is convergence – which brings me back to the octopus's eye."

"I'm glad you've got there, because this fellow is winning this staring competition," admits Milton. He has just blinked. The octopus is smirking.

"The idea behind convergence is that there are only so many ways for some things to happen. Not all biological forms are good for flight, or swimming, or even seeing."

"OK. I get that – it's like designing a plane. You don't make it like a concrete box because that would never reach lift off."

"Except we aren't talking about an engineer designing it here – it is more a case of self-organizing by the organism. It's as if the plane – or generations of planes – can come up with the solution themselves due to some deeper structural principles."

"That's so curious!"

"Isn't it? Take the eye. Humans have a camera-lens eye. So does an octopus. But 600 million years ago, the common ancestor to humans and octopuses didn't have this. It likely had eyespots. Humans and octopuses arrived at the camera-lens eye independently. In fact, so far biologists have counted seven separate evolutions of this kind of eye."[9]

That reminds Milton of a joke. "Harriet, what do you call a deer who hasn't got any eyes?"

Harriet sighs. "I don't know, what do you call a deer who hasn't got any eyes?"

"No idea – no-eye deer – get it?"

"I'm not sure you are listening to me, Milton."

"I am. Camera-lens eyes are a good solution to seeing and it has popped up seven times in different creatures. What about me? How do I see?" He poses so she can admire his fine eyes.

"You have a reflective eye, which makes it really good at seeing in low light conditions. I have eyes on the side of my head, rather than facing forward, which is good for spotting predators. Insects have compound eyes – which means lots of lenses, like in a dragonfly. We are examples of the main forms that have evolved. You see, there are different ways of seeing but there are limits to the number of structures that prove successful."

"So to fly a spaceship across the galaxy, it would be helpful to have a camera-lens eye and hands to use controls?" muses Milton.

"As far as we can imagine such a thing, then yes. Though this is a theory that hasn't yet been tested."

"It certainly helps though, when casting human actors in all those sci-fi films!" suggests Milton. "They don't have to go far from the basic human form."

They leave the octopus and head back to the time machine.

"Let me go over that again," says Milton. "Biologists agree that Darwin's Theory of Evolution is a good explanation. Some emphasize that evolution is completely random, but some now think there might be some trends and limits in the deeper

9 There is a fascinating discussion of this with Simon Conway Morris at https://www. whyarewehere.tv/our-universe/convergence/

structure of biological organisms that mean it converges on the same solutions to similar problems, such as seeing."

"Well done: you've followed that really well."

"I may not be able to outstare an octopus but I have two very excellent ears!"

"Simon Conway Morris says he agrees with Richard Dawkins, the famous atheistic science writer, who says that biology is blind to the outcomes, but Conway Morris goes on to say that it doesn't mean that the system isn't predisposed to life. He describes evolution as the mechanism by which the universe becomes self-aware – that means you and me asking curious questions about it. That's what we were talking about when we tackled the meaning of quantum physics for our place in the universe. I've been thinking about what you said and I agree that the Curious Quest is one of the things that gives value to our role in the universe. So what do you think now about evolution: random or convergence?"

Milton rubs his reflective eyes thoughtfully. He's feeling very challenged by all this. "I think I need to think a little longer about this before deciding."

"That's a very good answer. As biologists work on this in the future, they are going to be asking the same kind of big picture questions, and what they find out should be very exciting!"

Space–the Final Frontier!

Milton is still deep in thought. The Curious Quest has continued to amaze him but also encouraged him that he can understand things he thought beyond him. The universe is vast, but he has discovered on this journey with Harriet that it can also be understood in small steps as they travelled from Greeks, to Copernicus, to Galileo, to the Herschels, and now to the twentieth century.

"You know where I most want to go in our adventure?" he asks as they arrive back in the time machine.

"Where?" asks Harriet, presenting him with the scarf he helped rescue when she got into knots. She has knitted in a pattern of stars. "This is to say thank you for travelling with me."

"It's magnificent!" Milton admires his gift in the porthole glass. It sits around his neck like an astronaut's helmet. "I was wondering if we could go to see the race to space! I've always wanted to see the moon landing in 1969."

"What are our options?" asks Milton, curling up in a chair with his new scarf. He is secretly pleased to find Harriet back to her old self after her quantum wobble.

"We could go back to the very beginning," she muses. "We have a time machine."

Milton almost falls out of his chair. "Go and see the Big Bang?"

She laughs. "Not quite that far back! But that is a very interesting story."

GEORGES LEMAÎTRE, FATHER OF THE BIG BANG

- Lived: 1894–1966
- Number of jobs: 3 (Roman Catholic priest, astronomer, physics professor)
- Influence (out of 100): 83 (this Belgian astronomer was the first to argue that the universe was expanding and that it had originated in a "primeval atom" or "Cosmic Egg" – a theory we now know as the Big Bang. His influence was held back initially because many more famous physicists, including Einstein, didn't like the idea at first)
- Right? (out of 20): 20 (spot on! His theory of an expanding universe was quickly backed up by the observations of Edwin Hubble)
- Helpfully wrong? (out of 10): 0 (so far his theories have been proved correct)
- Interesting fact: in 1951, the Pope claimed that Lemaître's theory gave scientific proof for Catholicism. Tricky though it was to disagree with his boss, Lemaître pointed out that his theory was neutral, not proving or disproving religion. He opposed mixing science and religion. He believed the two were not in conflict with each other but were different kinds of knowledge.

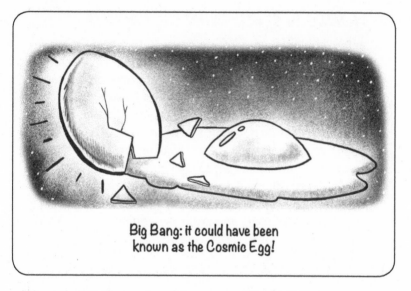

Big Bang: it could have been
known as the Cosmic Egg!

"If not the Big Bang, what did you mean?" asks Milton.

"I was talking about flight. We can't go straight to the moon without seeing how humans first left the earth in aircraft. We haven't touched on that yet." She polishes the face of one of the dials. "It's not really my area, as I have my feet close to the ground most of the time. I think we'd better go to visit an expert."

"Who's that? A rocket scientist?"

"No, an astronaut. I thought you'd like to meet Miss Baker, the first monkey to survive a space flight in 1959. We'll ask her to tell us about flying."

ANIMALS IN SPACE: RIGHT OR WRONG?

Before humans were sent into space, both the Russian and American space programmes experimented by launching rockets with animals on-board. Many species were used, from monkeys to dogs and cats, and even tortoises. The first to achieve orbit was Laika, a dog, launched in Sputnik 2. She died during the flight. At that stage the scientists had not worked out how to land the spacecraft, so she was never expected to live.

Our curiosity leads to some difficult questions. They were testing if space travel was safe for humans. What do you think about using animals in experiments where you know they will not survive?

Harriet lands the time machine in the US Space and Rocket Center in Alabama, a magnificent museum dedicated to space exploration. It's 1969, the height of the space race, when both the Soviet Union and the USA are vying to be the first to land on the moon. The Soviet Union has been ahead for most of the decade. Our two time travellers find Miss Baker, a squirrel monkey, is a star attraction at the museum in her retirement from being an astronaut.

"Miss Baker," calls Harriet. "Do you have a moment?"

The monkey leaps across her enclosure. "Harriet! It's been a long time!"

Milton wonders just how many adventures in the time machine Harriet had before they started travelling together.

"This is my friend, Milton," says Harriet. "We were wondering if you could tell us about the history of space flight."

"I can do better than that – I can show you."

Miss Baker lets herself out of her enclosure (she's been into space and back – locks aren't a challenge!). She leads them around the exhibits, starting with the Montgolfier hot air balloon.

1783: first manned
balloon flight, Paris

1903: first powered flight,
North Carolina

World War I: first fighting
planes

1927: Charles Lindbergh
crosses Atlantic

1933: first modern airliner

1937: Frank Whittle's jet engine

1939: Igor Sikorsky's helicopter

1957: the Soviet Union launches
first Sputnik (a manmade satellite)

1961: Yuri Gagarin, first
man in space

1963: Valentina
Tereshkova, first woman
in space

1969: US Apollo 11
moon landing

"Though all the visitors remember the names of the first astronauts Yuri Gargarin, Valentina Tereshkova, and Alan Shepard, none of these would have made it into space without thousands of scientists and engineers working to get them there," says Miss Baker. "And it is a real struggle for some of the people in the team to be recognized for their work."

"Like who?" asks Milton.

"Like Katherine Johnson." Miss Baker jumps on top of a model of the first Apollo rocket. "Did you know that before digital computers were introduced, a computer used to mean a person who did the maths?"

"No, but I suppose that follows," says Harriet.

"It was regarded as a boring task and so given to women like you'd give typing to a secretary." Miss Baker pulls a disgusted face. "In fact, it was crucial work. One mistake could spell disaster. At the American space agency, NASA, many of these women computers were African American and, in the late 1950s when I was there, these ladies were treated even worse than their white colleagues under a system called segregation – which meant they were kept apart."

"How horrible!" mews Milton.

"But my heroine, Katherine Johnson, changed that. She was so good at the maths of orbital mechanics that she busted through these barriers to become the first woman to be brought onto the rocket scientists' team. She forced people to look at her skill, not her colour. She was crucial to calculating the flight of the first American astronaut, Alan Shepard, finding the right launch window for his rocket. Even after digital computers were introduced at NASA, the first American in orbit, John Glenn, refused to fly unless Katherine Johnson checked the figures."

"I don't blame him. I think I'd also trust her over a new-fangled machine!" says Harriet.

"And you know what they're doing today?" asks Miss Baker. "They are going to the moon! Katherine Johnson has been part of the team working on that too."

"Would you like to go to watch?" asks Harriet.

"I'd love to – but my flying days are over. They won't want me there."

"But we want you as our co-pilot in our time machine. As you were the first monkey in orbit, I think you should be at the moon landing too. You helped get them there with your own bravery."

Put like that, Miss Baker leaps at the chance. "What are we waiting for?"

MEET THE SCIENTIST

JOCELYN BELL BURNELL
AND PULSAR STARS

Katherine Johnson isn't the only woman involved in space science who has been overlooked. Jocelyn Bell Burnell is an astrophysicist, but her story does raise questions about how female scientists have been treated even in relatively recent times.

- Lived: Born in 1943
- Number of jobs: 3 (astrophysicist, Chancellor of University of Dundee, President of Royal Society of Edinburgh)
- Influence (out of 100): 45 (credit for her work on pulsars was given mainly to her supervisor)
- Right? (out of 20): 16 (while a postgraduate student studying under Antony Hewish and with astronomer Martin Ryle, she was the first to discover a pulsar – a highly magnetic kind of star that gives out a beam of electromagnetic radiation. If the beam is pointed at earth, the radio wave that comes from these stars is received in a regular pattern, a little like the beam from a lighthouse. At first Jocelyn and her colleagues joked that it could be extraterrestrial so nicknamed the signal LGM-1 (or Little Green Men!). They changed this when another pulsar was discovered as they realized they had proof it had a natural origin)
- Helpfully wrong? (out of 10): 8 (the joke about LGM shows that even when scientists are playfully "wrong" – the researchers knew that there was only ever the slightest chance extraterrestrials were involved – they can still have fun!)

- Interesting facts: in 1974, Hewish and Ryle were both awarded the Nobel Prize for Physics with no mention of Bell Burnell, despite the fact that she was the first to spot a pulsar. She graciously said that it was because she was a postgraduate student, but many still think it unfair and that her gender played a role in her being overlooked. In 2018 she won the Special Breakthrough Prize in Fundamental Physics, worth £2.3 million, for her discovery of radio pulsars. She donated all of the money to fund women, under-represented ethnic minorities and refugees to become physics researchers. Go Jocelyn!

Harriet pilots the time machine to the launch site at the Kennedy Space Center. A huge white rocket stands supported by a framework called a gantry. At a safe distance, a crowd has gathered to watch.

"Thirty seconds and counting!" declares Mission Control.

Unnoticed by the crowd, Harriet, Milton, and Miss Baker slip out of the box and take a prime spot to watch. It is a bright sunny day with a cloudless sky: perfect for a launch.

"I feel good about this," says the monkey. "The launch is one of the most dangerous parts of the mission, but the signs are promising."

"I feel optimistic too," says Milton, winking at Harriet.

"Twelve, eleven, ten, nine, ignition sequence starts…" comes the announcement. As they watch, a great billow of fire erupts under the rocket – the fuel burning to produce the power to launch it. "Six, five, four, three, two, one, zero, all engines running, lift off – we have lift off!"

Everyone cheers and applauds as they follow the rocket's rapid rise into the sky. Milton is moved by the sight; he wipes a tear away with his paw. "It's so beautiful!"

"Isn't it?" agrees Miss Baker. "Inside the rocket, though, it isn't so pretty. The astronauts will be experiencing G-force – the pressure you feel as you accelerate to escape the gravitational pull of the earth. It's not very comfortable."

The rocket makes a successful separation from its extra fuel tanks and clears the atmosphere.

"That's the first part over. Now the new challenge: to land on the moon!" says Miss Baker. "I do so hope they succeed."

"Shall we go there to watch them?" suggests Harriet. "I'm sure I can find a quiet spot to park."

Her companions need no further persuading. They set off, following the Apollo 11 mission into space. They've no need to hurry as it will take the astronauts three days to get there.

GETTING A MOVE ON IN PLATE TECTONICS

While Harriet, Milton, and Miss Baker prepare for the moon landing, they will be looking out of the window back at the earth. What do they see? A beautiful blue planet with intriguingly shaped continents. They also see it very differently from how it would have looked millions of years ago. Until the nineteenth century, the earth was thought to be fixed – that the seas, landmasses, and all their smaller features had been in place since the earth was formed. As geologists gathered more facts about what was going on under the surface, they challenged old ideas about the age of the earth. A surprising new thought pushed up through the age-old crust of assumptions.

What if the earth itself wasn't as stable as we thought?

Back in the sixteenth century when people first began to draw up accurate maps of the continents of Africa and South America, it was noticed that they "fitted" together.

Odd, hey?

Then the discoveries about radioactive decay gave more accurate clues to the age of the earth. Scientists realized that it was both older than had been thought and still sufficiently hot to have a liquid core.

Hmm – interesting.

Then in 1912 a German geologist called Alfred Wegener came up with the idea that the continents might have drifted over vast periods of time into their current positions. Others had suggested this before but he backed up the theory of continental drift with geological evidence; for example, that the rocks in Scotland and Ireland were very similar to those found in Newfoundland and New Brunswick in Canada, as you would expect if these two regions, now separated by the Atlantic, had once been joined.

Clever!

Too clever for some. Wegener met with opposition, in part because he couldn't explain how that happened. He died on an expedition to the Arctic in 1930 before he could provide an answer.

Other scientists suggested in the years that followed that the earth's surface was divided into different fragments, or tectonic plates. In places, the plates moved apart, creating new ocean basins; in others, they pushed together, building new mountain belts and chains of volcanoes. More discoveries helped everyone agree on continental drift. Geologists spotted that the magnetic fields in rock layers changed direction and strength, suggesting movement in the earth, and from the 1950s they had much better data on the ocean floor too. An American geologist, Marie Tharp, and her colleague, Bruce Heezen, produced a detailed map of the seabed that helped show what was going on. Their map revealed a huge underwater Mid-Atlantic Ridge, showing where there was a chain of active volcanoes under the sea.

Everyone's big picture of how the earth was formed had to change as a result of plate tectonics. Instead of an earth formed once and staying the same, it was now understood that over a huge expanse of time, the earth too changed.

And it also gave answers to why we have clusters of high mountains, volcanoes, and earthquakes in some regions – it's all to do with moving plates!

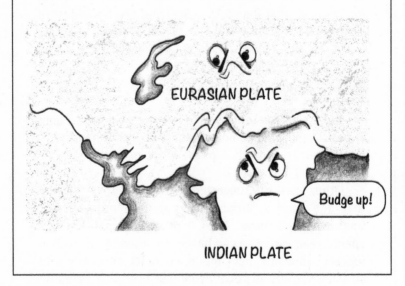

Nipping ahead of Apollo 11 on the landing day, Harriet finds a convenient crater in which to hide the time machine. "If you look in the wardrobe, you'll find spacesuits," she tells them.

"We're going outside?" asks Milton. "Cool!"

"But you remember about gravity, don't you?" Harriet says. "As the moon is smaller than the earth, it has a smaller gravitational pull."

Milton isn't listening. He's dressed and out of the door.

"Whee!" he cries as he leaps from rock to rock. "It's like being on a trampoline but better!"

"Milton, come back! We can't have paw prints all over the moon for when the astronauts get here."

Agreeing that this would be a bad idea, Milton quickly scuffs over the prints he has made with a swipe of his tail. He does this just in time because the lunar module, *Eagle,* has separated from the command vessel, *Columbia.* That command craft is piloted by Michael Collins and will eventually take them home. For now though, the *Eagle* is rapidly approaching its landing site.

"Who's in there?" asks Miss Baker.

"Astronauts Neil Armstrong and Buzz Aldrin," replies Harriet.

"How do they decide who gets to go outside first, I wonder?" muses Miss Baker.

"Flip a coin?" suggests Milton.

"That's hard in low gravity and now they're a bit busy landing the spacecraft," says Miss Baker.

"I think Neil Armstrong is closest to the exit," says Harriet. "He's also the senior officer. He's the one to go first. I hope he's got some suitable words to say: this is quite a moment for humankind."

Bouncing across the powdery surface of the moon, they crouch behind a rock. Though the sky is black, they can see no stars as the daylight is so bright. Light bounces off every pale surface. A ladder emerges from the *Eagle* and an astronaut makes his way down. Milton feels a thrill of excitement go down his spine.

"Wow!" he mews.

"That's one small step for man," says Armstrong, his white suit glowing in the sunlight. "One giant leap for mankind."

Buzz Aldrin follows. "Beautiful view," he says.

Milton has to agree: the earth is rising over the moon's surface. From here, our planet is a swirl of clouds over the blue seas and grey-green lands. He sighs with happiness.

"We'd better go before they spot us," whispers Harriet.

As they leave the two astronauts exploring the moon's surface, they see them plant an American flag and pose for photos.

Wriggling out of her spacesuit, Miss Baker goes back to the porthole. "I feel sorry for Michael Collins left up in *Columbia*. He didn't get to set foot on the moon."

"They couldn't do it without him," says Harriet. "Scientific exploration isn't about the famous names; it's a team effort. They couldn't have done it without you, Miss Baker – or all the thousands of researchers, number crunchers, and even the politicians who voted for the money to pay for the space programme."

"I know. Thank you for letting me join your team today," says Miss Baker. "I'd better get back before the museum notices I'm gone."

"Don't worry. We can get you back moments after you left," says Milton.

"You won't even miss dinner," promises Harriet.

WHERE NEXT FOR SPACE TRAVEL?

Since the moon landing in 1969, scientific exploration has continued, often thanks to unpiloted craft that can travel where humans can't (yet!). Here are some of the highlights:

- **Viking 1 and 2** were probes that landed on Mars in the 1970s. These were followed by Mars Global Surveyor, which mapped the surface in 1997, and Spirit and Opportunity, which landed in 2004.

• **Voyager 1** launched in 1977. It has travelled further than any other manufactured object, having flown past Jupiter and Saturn, and is heading out of our solar system.

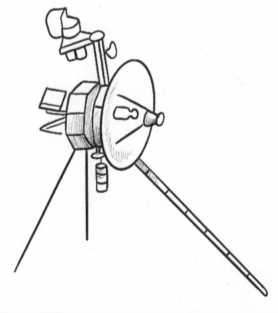

- The **Space Shuttle programme**: 1981 sees the launch of a reusable spacecraft, *Columbia*. The programme lasted for 135 missions (sadly including two major disasters with the loss of fourteen lives) until 2011. In that time, space shuttles carried the Hubble telescope into space and helped construct the International Space Station.

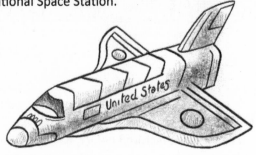

- The **Hubble Space Telescope** was launched to orbit in 1990. This telescope does not have to look through the earth's atmosphere so is able to send us amazing images of deep space. You can see what it is looking at right now if you go to http://hubblesite.org

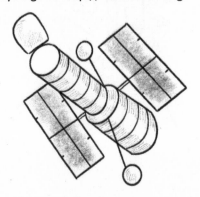

- Launched in 1997, the **Cassini** mission to Saturn lasted two decades. You can find out what it did and see some amazing pictures of the ringed planet here: https://saturn.jpl.nasa.gov

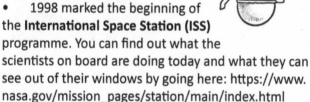

- 1998 marked the beginning of the **International Space Station (ISS)** programme. You can find out what the scientists on board are doing today and what they can see out of their windows by going here: https://www.nasa.gov/mission_pages/station/main/index.html

- The **Kepler Space Telescope** – sent into space in 2009, this observatory has confirmed the existence of lots of planets outside our solar system orbiting stars. It has shown there is no such thing as a typical solar system. Some planets orbit two suns, and astronomers even detected one that orbits three! Kepler has reached the end of its life since it ran out of fuel.

- **Mars mission**: both NASA and private company SpaceX are looking into a manned mission to Mars. There are huge technical challenges to overcome but NASA is currently planning to send astronauts to orbit Mars and return to earth in the 2030s. Maybe you'll be part of the team of scientists to make this possible?

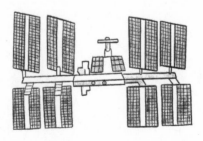

WHERE NEXT FOR SCIENCE?

After leaving Miss Baker at her home, Milton and Harriet look through their souvenirs from their Curious Quest. They have a paintbrush from a prehistoric cave, a Greek play, a star chart from the Islamic Golden Age, fragments of medieval stained glass, a page from the first printed book, a crystal from Isaac Newton's study, a fossil from Mary Anning, a seashell from the Galapagos, and many other treasures. Milton adds a packet of freeze-dried ice cream made for astronauts. They know it is nearly time for them to go home too but they aren't quite ready to stop.

"Can we go ahead to the Mars mission, Harriet?" asks Milton. "I'd really like to see that."

"Maybe *we* can, but we can't tell anyone about it," she says.

"Why not?"

"If the people following our mission through our reports know the future, we might change what happens."

"That's another of those paradoxes, isn't it?" grumbles Milton. "So what *can* we show them?"

"I think we can show them the future in what scientists are doing today."

Milton crosses his eyes at that statement. "Pardon?"

"I think we should look at the most promising areas for scientific exploration, the ones we think are going to have the biggest effect on tomorrow. We should come up with one each – a competition to find the best area."

"I understand now. That sounds fun," agrees Milton. "Let's take a few minutes to think about it."

They go to opposite sides of the time machine. Milton curls up into his thinking ball, head tucked into his body. Harriet vanishes inside her shell. All they can hear are the whirs and clicks of the time machine.

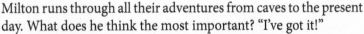

TRY THIS AT HOME

You've been on the Curious Science Quest with Harriet and Milton. What do you think are the three most important areas of science going forward into the future?

Now read on and see if Harriet and Milton agree with you!

Milton runs through all their adventures from caves to the present day. What does he think the most important? "I've got it!"

Harriet emerges. "Me too. Let's write them down. No peeking!"

Milton quickly scribbles his:

COOL NEW MATERIALS FOR MAKING THINGS

Harriet writes hers in her beautiful curling script.

Ways to combat climate change

There's a whirr and a ping from the time machine. It doesn't want to be left out.

ARTIFICIAL INTELLIGENCE

Working in two dimensions: graphene

"That's settled then. For our last adventure, we are going to fly past these three areas and see which is going to have the biggest impact," says Harriet. "We'll look at your cool inventions first, Milton. That means a trip to Manchester, England." Harriet turns around but sees that the machine is already programming itself. "Oh!"

The machine posts a message for her on its display. "Never underestimate my intelligence!"

"I think the machine is making a point," says Milton. "Soon we won't be needed. But why Manchester?"

"Because in 2004 two researchers, Andre Geim and Konstantin Novoselov, made the first two-dimensional, or 2D, material – graphene."

"How can it be 2D? Don't we live in a 3D world?"

"That's because it is only one atom thick – and that's very, very thin. It is almost as if it is 2D."

The time travellers arrive at Manchester University. They sneak into a laboratory in search of the two scientists.

"I bet they are using very impressive kit for their experiments," whispers Milton.

"We'll see," says Harriet with a smile.

They creep up behind the physicists and find them…

"They're playing with sticky tape!" exclaims Milton.

"I know. Isn't it funny to think that the most promising new material was discovered by the same stuff we use to wrap birthday presents?"

"That's good," says Andre, looking at his latest sample of tape. "I think we're right. Each layer we peel from this block of graphite is just one atom thick."

"A playful idea is perfect to start things," says Konstantin. "Now comes the serious work. I wonder what we can do with it?"

"The structure will look something like this," says Andre. He draws on the white board.

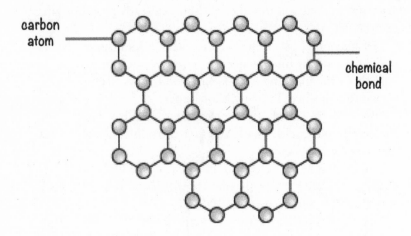

"That's going to make it extremely strong," says Konstantin.

"And the electrons are going to be able to move very quickly so it will be a great conductor of electricity. I can see we've got our work cut out finding out all these possible uses."

Harriet and Milton leave the scientists to get down to their exciting new material and return to the time machine.

"Graphene does turn out to be the thinnest and strongest material known to science – a hundred times stronger than steel," says Harriet. "And they are right: there are so many uses. It conducts electricity but is flexible and transparent. Think of all the new electronic devices that will be able to use it."

"Even smarter smartphones?" suggests Milton. "If it's flexible, maybe we'll have ones we can bend and fold?"

"Or wear like clothes. And the good thing is that it is carbon-based, and carbon is the basic element of life. Perhaps it can be made biodegradable – that's good news for the environment. And maybe we'll have even faster computers too."

Milton is reading up on graphene on the computer. "It says here that we could use it to take salt out of seawater because it can act as a filter. That's a really big help for countries in drought."

"It is so light and strong that it will make vehicles much lighter and so use less fuel. That's another way it could help combat climate change. It can even help clear up nuclear waste as graphene can be used to bind contaminants into clumps for removal."

"Hang on a minute, Harriet. How come we've gone from talking about my cool new inventions to your area of climate change?" Milton is suspicious that she's been steering the quest in her favour.

Harriet shrugs. "I didn't plan this, Milton, but it does go to show that areas of science are so interlinked these days, you can't help finding things that cut across the old boundaries. You can't really say something is more important than another area because they all depend on each other, like pillars holding up a bridge. Time for my pick. Let's go and see a place where they are trying to counter climate change."

WHAT IS MEANT BY CLIMATE CHANGE?

Climate change is the large-scale change in the earth's weather patterns and temperatures. The earth's climate has always changed over time, but since the mid to late twentieth century the process has sped up to a dangerous level. The scientific community agrees that human activity, especially the burning of fossil fuels, is driving the change. How is that having an effect? The release of carbon dioxide and other greenhouse gases from the fuel traps the sun's heat like glass in a greenhouse, and so warms the earth's atmosphere. The rising temperature has knock-on effects on the sea and polar ice caps. The result might soon be no ice during the summer in the Arctic and rising sea levels as the ice melts into the oceans. The concern is that the longer we leave it to change our ways, the more difficult it will be to put on the brakes and stop the temperature rising any further.

We saw this process start in *Victorian Voyages* with the Industrial Revolution.[10] It is up to people in our time to solve the problem with a new green revolution.

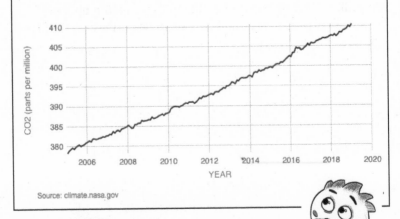

Source: climate.nasa.gov

10   See Harriet and Milton's adventure down a coal mine in *Victorian Voyages*.

"Where do you have in mind?" Milton asks.

"Combating climate change is everyone's responsibility, so it's happening all over the globe," says Harriet. "The best thing we can do is stop using so much energy and recycle where we can. But people are also developing new sources of power from renewables like wind, water, and sun, to nuclear energy, and new biofuels – that's fuel made from quick-growing natural products like crops and even algae."

"That's a long list," replies Milton. "I think we should investigate a renewable source of power. Let's allow the time machine to pick our destination."

"Time Machine," says Harriet, "please take us to the biggest solar power plant on earth in 2018."

No problem.

Milton watches the world fly by. "Isn't this extra exciting, not knowing where we are going? I think it must be in America."

"I'm guessing China," says Harriet.

They are both wrong. The time machine lands in India, in Tamil Nadu state, which is in the south. The machine has sent a message ahead and organized for someone to show them around.

The door opens and a trunk wiggles in to shake paws.

"Welcome to India," says a young Indian elephant, standing outside the box. "My name is Sabeen and I will be your guide for this visit."

"An elephant! Why an elephant?" Milton asks the time machine.

Because they never forget…

"True."

And the plant is 10 square kilometres, so you might like someone to carry you.

"Also true. Thank you. You really are clever."

The machine whirrs with pleasure.

Sabeen lifts Harriet up onto her broad back and Milton scrambles aboard, making sure not to prick her with his claws.

"Ready?" asks Sabeen. "Hold on. We have a long way to go."

As she plods along the narrow paths between the solar panels, she begins her commentary. "What you can see are two and a half million solar panels producing energy. We can make enough electricity to power the homes of three-quarters of a million people. As India will soon have the largest population of any country, we have to find ways of supplying them that don't harm the world's climate. This is one part of the answer."

"So you get the input for free because it is the sun?" says Milton, remembering not to look directly up at the sun as it beats overhead.

"And even better, it will not run out like fossil fuels. Only one ten millionth of the sun's energy reaches the earth's surface. Just ninety minutes of that is equal to all the power used by humans in a year. The limitation isn't on the supply, it's on capturing it. Can you guess what limits us?" Sabeen asks.

TRY THIS AT HOME: LIMITS TO SOLAR POWER

It's your turn to think like a scientist. What do you think are the main things that stop us supplying all our needs from solar power?

Now let's see what Sabeen, Harriet, and Milton have to say and see if you're right.

"Hmm, I imagine night-time is a problem," says Harriet.

"And clouds. I know it's sunny now but even here you must have rain and storms, surely?" suggests Milton.

"Yes, we do," agrees the elephant.

"So unless you have a way of storing the energy for those times, you can't control how much electricity you provide for the grid," concludes Harriet.

"Scientists are working on the storage problem and may come up with some answers soon," says Sabeen. "But we have another problem because we are a hot dry place. Can you guess?"

Milton's nose is itching. Sabeen's big feet are stirring up the dry ground. That's it! "Dust!"

"Correct, little cat. One of the biggest jobs here is keeping the panels clean."

"Do you use your trunk to squirt them?"

Sabeen curls her trunk up over her head and tickles him. "Oh no – that's too much work even for a big creature like me. Besides, we don't use water as that is a precious resource. We have a special dusting device, a little like the soft spinning brushes you see in a car wash. They run over the panels to keep them in tip-top working order."

The travellers stop to have tea with Sabeen near the building that houses the equipment that turns the electricity from the solar panels into electricity for the grid.

"I think we really are seeing the future here," says Milton as he gazes at the rank upon rank of solar panels.

"Especially for sunny countries," agrees Harriet. "Thank you for showing us your solar farm, Sabeen."

"Come back any time." She raises her trunk in farewell.

Just as Milton is about to follow Harriet into the time machine, he gets blasted with a cool spray of water. "Hey!"

Sabeen chuckles and trumpets her farewell.

"Cheeky! I'll get you back next time!" Milton promises.

Shaking off his fur, Milton finds Harriet standing over the control desk.

"Time Machine, where do you want us to go to see an example of artificial intelligence?" she asks politely.

It is everywhere in modern life. Search engines. Social networks. Streaming services. But they are no fun to show you.

"OK, says Milton. "Let's go somewhere fun then!"

Buckle up!

That sounds a little alarming, but Harriet and Milton do as it says and put on their safety belts. The machine jumps from India to…

A racetrack. The car they have landed in is going fast but…

"Hey, Harriet, where's the driver?" squeaks Milton. He reaches out to take over but then sees that the steering is moving smoothly on its own.

The vehicle is driving itself.

"This is only an experimental model. It uses machine learning to improve on how it drives. Guess what the biggest problem it has on the roads is."

"Bumps and sudden turns?" suggests Harriet.

"Other drivers?" says Milton.

"Correct. The biggest problem for driverless cars is the unpredictable behaviour of humans both in cars and as pedestrians. Artificial intelligence hasn't quite cracked that code yet."

Now Milton sees that the car is well under control on this racetrack, he begins to enjoy the ride. "So in the future, we might not have to do some of the things we take for granted today: drive cars…"

"Diagnose some kinds of illnesses – machines are learning to do that too," adds Harriet.

"Work out what we want to watch or listen to next. An algorithm tailored to us can decide for us." Milton pauses. "Wait a moment! Isn't that a bit dangerous? First our lives will be run by a machine and the next step will be the machines taking over. Do scientific advances mean that we won't be needed for science any longer? That robots and other machines will be able to carry on without us?"

Artificial intelligence could spell the end of the human race. It could take off on its own, and redesign itself at an ever increasing rate.

Harriet presses the button to disengage the autopilot and takes over driving the car. She brings it safely to the side of the track. "That's why we need to listen to warnings from the physicists Professor Hawking, Lord Rees, and many others. That's one of the things this quest has been about. We must always ask questions about where our curiosity is taking us and make sure we approve of where it is going before it is too late. We explored over the centuries how science mostly travelled well in the slipstream of those asking the ultimate questions in philosophy and faith. Maybe we can say now that science *needs* to travel in the slipstream of other knowledge, like religious and ethical values, so that technology doesn't cause a crash and wipe out everything we value."

"I don't want to live in a world where machines take over," agrees Milton. "I want to live in a world where we explore the wonder of the universe and take care of the world as best we can."

With a smile, Harriet plots a course back to where they started.

"Do you remember what question started us on this quest, Milton?" asks Harriet. "Back before we went to the caves in our first adventure?"

"Oh yes. I told you that I thought these were odd words to have over a modern laboratory door. I also said faith and science didn't go together and that there was no proof any god made the universe." Milton wonders now how he could've been so certain about all that!

"And what do you think now?"

Milton licks his paws. This is very deep stuff and needs thinking about carefully. "I think I understand now why these words are here. They mean that the universe is amazing and it is fun to find out about it – and I've discovered that everyone can do that. All of us are curious. We saw that right back with the cave painters."

"And what about God and creation?" asks Harriet.

"On our journey, I think I've seen that science can't prove this either way as science isn't able to answer that sort of question. That doesn't mean that science and faith are completely separate for everyone. Some people believe the universe was created by God, and that gives them a hunger to find out more about all the world he made for us."

Harriet nods. "Yes, people like Isaac Newton, William and Caroline Herschel, Mary Anning, Michael Faraday, James Clerk Maxwell, and Francis Collins – they've all thought, or think, that. For them, their scientific questions travelled in the slipstream created by their belief in God. Faith really helped them on their own curious quest."

"But a lot of people are uncertain like me," adds Milton. "Even if you don't think you can know if God exists or not, or aren't sure what he might be like, you'll probably agree it is a pretty cool universe we live in and is worth exploring. That's the kind of thinking we saw with Charles Darwin, Marie Skłowdowska-Curie, and Albert Einstein, isn't it?"

"I believe so. And, of course, some reject the idea of God

completely, such as the discoverers of the structure of DNA, Francis Crick and James Watson, and the science writer Richard Dawkins. But they love asking scientific questions too and find wonder in it all. So what do you think that means, Milton?"

Milton knows what he thinks about that – after visiting over three thousand years of science. "That science is for everyone, no matter your world view. But you shouldn't try to make science or religion answer each other's questions because that's when the uh-oh moments happen."

"Very wise. You don't want to be too sure you already know everything or it might blind you to the real answers. That was what happened when people refused to listen to what Philoponus and Galileo were telling them."

"But the story doesn't end there, does it?" says Milton. "We've seen in our modern flights that you need to think beyond the laboratory when you have a really tricky question about what to do with what you've found out, like with nuclear physics and artificial intelligence. Science can't ride alone. We need help from other sources of wisdom to make difficult choices." Milton is very pleased with himself at coming to this conclusion.

"I think that's a very good point, Milton. You can't answer ultimate questions about the meaning and purpose of life just from science. I think you've definitely earned a reward trip. Shall we slip away to the future to see the Mars landing?"

Milton's ears prick up. "Will there be snacks?"

"I've got some sardines and lettuce packed, so we're ready to go."

He turns to look out at you, the reader. "What about the people who've been following our reports?"

"Oh, they'll get there too, but the relatively slow way!" says Harriet. "Come on, Milton. Our Curious Quest is far from over!"

The time travellers wave goodbye and return to the time machine. In a blink of an eye they are gone into the future, flying through time and space.

Where to go to find out more

Sources

You can check out our Science Has The Best Stories YouTube channel to find out more from leading scientists and artists who are inspired by science. It also has some more "Try this at Home" experiments: **https://www.youtube.com/channel/UCkgKDWT0_hUR3QdPu8ck2nA**

This Dominic Walliman video is an excellent introduction to quantum physics: **https://www.youtube.com/watch?v=ARWBdfWpDyc**

For more information about the Large Hadron Collider, watch this Oxford Sparks animation: **https://www.youtube.com/watch?v=BEnaEMMAO_s**

This interview with Professor Ard Louis on the Science Has The Best Stories channel has more information about self-organizing by the organism: **https://youtu.be/BHhn0PafGdU**

Here is some footage of the Apollo 11 mission, whose launch Harriet and Milton attended in chapter 4: **https://www.youtube.com/watch?v=N9tIX5-dq3E**

If you want to find out more about Katherine Johnson and the other brilliant African-American women at NASA, watch *Hidden Figures* (2016), a film about their role in the space programme.

For more information about graphene, watch the video at the University of Manchester's graphene site: **https://www.graphene.manchester.ac.uk**

Answers

How many times did you spot the Curiosity Bug? The answer is 16.

Harriet and Milton would like to thank...

Professor Paul Davies, Professor George Ellis, Professor Emmanuel Tsesmelis, Professor Ard Louis, and Professor Bob White (who helped us while he was on a volcano on La Reunion).

They would also like to thank Brett Hudson, their illustrator, the team at Lion Children's Books (especially Deborah Lock, Jacqui Crawford, Fern Lindsey-Tolland, Margaret Milton, and Kirsten Etheridge), Amelia Knight at Midas PR, and Lynne Humphries, who all helped bring these books from an idea to completion.

More thanks to those who spent some of their valuable time reading and then giving their backing to the series, including the Most Reverend Justin Welby, Professor Rebecca Fitzgerald, Professor Rolf Heuer, Reverend Dr Malcolm Guite, Bob Hartman, Dr Allan Chapman, and Lord Rees.

And finally, Julia, Andrew, and Roger would like to thank their families, especially Joss, Diana, and Annie, for supporting them on this trip through time.

Meet the authors

Julia Golding is a multi-award-winning children's novelist, including the *Cat Royal* series, the *Companions Quartet*, and *The Curious Crime*. Having given up on science at sixteen, she became interested again when she realized just how inspiring science can be. It really does tell the best stories! This is her first experiment with non-fiction but hopefully her collaborators, Roger and Andrew, will prevent any laboratory accidents.

Andrew Briggs is the professor of nanomaterials at the University of Oxford. Nanomaterials just means small stuff. In his laboratory he studies problems like how electricity flows through a single molecule (you can't get stuff much smaller than a single molecule). He is also curious about big questions. He flies aeroplanes, but he has never been in a time travel machine like the one that Harriet and Milton use – yet!

Roger Wagner is an artist who paints power stations and angels (among other things) and has work in collections around the world. He didn't do the drawings for these books, but like Milton and Harriet he wanted to find out how the "big picture" thinking of artists was connected to what scientists do. When he met Andrew Briggs the two of them set out on a journey to answer that question. Their journey (which they described in a book called *The Penultimate Curiosity*) was almost (but not quite) as exciting as Milton and Harriet's.

You can see Roger and Andrew's adventure in a plane at **https://curiositystream.com/video/2047/the-penultimate-curiosity**.